Praise for *Preaching and the Human Condition*

"Preachers too often forget that sermons are elements of a spiritual marathon rather than a sprint. They focus on the impact of a single sermon instead of thinking about the tapestry they are weaving over time for their listeners. Week in and week out their sermons explore both the joys and the good news of the gospel, as well as suffering and sorrow of life. Given the cumulative nature of preaching, Allen reminds preachers they need to craft three-dimensional proclamations. Through their preaching marathon they explore the deep, inner woven deep structure of those three dimensions: the divine, the other, and the self. And Allen issues this central challenge to preachers—they are to take off their 'floaties,' step out of the baby pool, and dive into the deep end where God is waiting."
—Lucy Lind Hogan, Hugh Latimer Elderdice Professor of Preaching and Worship, Wesley Theological Seminary, Washington, DC

"O. Wesley Allen offers what may be the single best piece of homiletical advice I have yet encountered: 'get out of the baby pool and plunge into deeper water—focus more narrowly and swim more deeply.' There is no way that any one sermon can address or resolve any one aspect of the human condition, much less what Allen calls the physical, intellectual, psychological, spiritual, material, and social implications of the events in our daily lives that threaten or damage our well-being as humans. What preachers are invited to do in this book is bring a consciously cumulative approach to their preaching in which they begin to address these issues regularly and consistently over a long period of time. Allen urges preachers to think about the human condition vertically (God and humanity), horizontally (person-to-person), and inwardly (how sin damages but never destroys the imago dei in each of us). This book shines a light of compassion on every marginalized person and community, and it reminds the reader that as often as not we are both the victims and the causes of human suffering. That discovery may be the greatest irony of the human condition."
—Marvin A. McMickle, President, Cc   y
School

D1205848

"Wes Allen's overarching concern, which he reaffirms in every chapter of this book, is with 'the preacher's task of proclaiming how God's good news addresses the human condition.' It is a worthy concern, and he applies his incisive mind equally and perceptively to both sides of its demanding equation: to the good news and to the human condition. Allen keeps his eye firmly on God's saving action in Jesus Christ, while remaining utterly candid about the brokenness of human life. The result is a book that offers no easy answers but instead enables preachers to preach genuine Christian hope amid the realities of human striving and suffering and to shine a light on a path for faithful living."
—Thomas G. Long, Bandy Professor of Preaching, Emeritus, Candler School of Theology, Emory University

"Having spent two decades in pastoral ministry and several years serving alongside one of the best preachers alive, I wish someone had put this book in my hand years ago! I urge any preacher to read it and re-read it periodically. If you'll take this advice, the people you preach to will be significantly more engaged, impacted, and transformed by the gospel."
—Glen Shoup, Executive Pastor of Worship, The United Methodist Church of the Resurrection

PREACHING
and *the* HUMAN
CONDITION

Loving God, Self, & Others

O. WESLEY ALLEN, JR.

Abingdon Press
Nashville

PREACHING AND THE HUMAN CONDITION:
LOVING GOD, SELF, & OTHERS

Copyright © 2016 by Abingdon Press

Library of Congress Cataloging-in-Publication Data has been requested.

ISBN 978-1-5018-1890-5

Scripture quotations unless noted otherwise are from the Common English Bible. Copyright © 2011 by the Common English Bible. All rights reserved. Used by permission. www.CommonEnglishBible.com.

Scripture quotations marked (NRSV) are taken from the New Revised Standard Version of the Bible, copyright 1989, Division of Christian Education of the National Council of the Churches of Christ in the United States of America. Used by permission. All rights reserved.

16 17 18 19 20 21 22 23 24 25—10 9 8 7 6 5 4 3 2 1
MANUFACTURED IN THE UNITED STATES OF AMERICA

For
Ronald J. Allen,
who has offered me gracious support
throughout my entire career as a homiletician.
He has read
most of the books I have written
while they were in process and made them much better with his critique.
He has excelled as a mentor,
has served as a role model for me as a scholar and teacher,
is a tried and true friend,
and is one of the most authentic persons of faith I have ever met.
In language his and my scholarship share,
I could not be more grateful
that Ron has been one of my most valued
"conversation partners."

CONTENTS

ACKNOWLEDGMENTS

This book began as a lecture at Perkins School of Theology at Southern Methodist University as part of an interview process. It was completed approximately a year later, after Perkins had accepted me into their fold. I am grateful for the welcome the faculty gave to me and my early thoughts on this matter and especially for the support I have received from William Lawrence, dean; Evelyn Parker, associate dean for Academic Affairs; and Alyce McKenzie, my colleague in homiletics.

A number of people have graciously read through parts of this book for me at different stages of its evolution: professors Emily Askew, Jerry Sumney (Lexington Theological Seminary), and Ron Allen (Christian Theological Seminary); and pastors Sally Allocca (Birmingham, Alabama), Derek Penwell (Louisville, Kentucky), Dave Clark (Long Beach, California), and especially Ron Lucky (Lexington, Kentucky). Any flaws in the book and its argument are mine, but without the contributions of these conversation partners there would be many more. I am thankful for their help and their friendship.

Connie Stella and her colleagues at Abingdon Press have likewise improved the book at every turn, and I am thankful for the chance to work with them once again.

I completed this project in Christmastide of 2015. How fitting to put the final edits on a book on the human condition during the season in which we celebrate the Nativity, the story in which the church proclaims that God took on our humanity. Christ was born of a mortal woman, grew into adulthood, was tempted, dealt with conflicts, suffered, and died just like us . . . and experienced all of this for us. Along with all Christian preachers who struggle to bring God's good news to bear on the sins and suffering of humanity, I give thanks for Emmanuel, God-with-us.

A Cumulative Homiletical Approach to the Human Condition

[THE ONE] WHO WOULD SEARCH FOR PEARLS MUST DIVE BELOW.

—John Dryden

Early in the process of developing this book, my teenage daughter asked me about its topic. I told her the book was going to be about preachers addressing the human condition. Her only response was, "Well, what other condition would they address?"

She is right, of course. The topic I have chosen is so obvious one wonders why a book about it is needed at all. All sermons either address existential issues related to the human condition directly or deal with other theological topics (such as some aspect of the character of God or a theological understanding of creation) that have implications for the human condition.

That said, we preachers have not necessarily dealt with the human condition as best we could. A few years ago, my seminary faculty had its annual retreat at a nearby undergraduate institution. Part of the retreat involved meeting with a group of religious studies majors to help us get a sense of what kinds of undergraduate students might be heading toward graduate theological studies. One of the students mentioned that after coming to college, he quit attending worship regularly. Imagining that a pluralistic and sociological approach to religious studies had disillusioned him about the faith he once held as a naïve youth, one of my colleagues engaged him further on the matter. But the twenty-year-old said it was not that he did not believe in the Christian faith anymore. Indeed, his studies had led him, in his own assessment, to greater faith. The problem, he said, was that on Sunday mornings he rarely heard anything in the pulpit that he could not hear on *Oprah* on a weekday afternoon.[1] We all winced at the blatant truth he was willing to speak to us. Self-help, hortatory, or prosperity-gospel kinds of sermons that reflect the kind of content we find on afternoon talk shows are rarely built on the kind of critical, existential encounter with and analysis of the human condition that leads to the transformation of the lives of those in the pews.

The difficulty with addressing the human condition with appropriate depth, of course, is nothing new. For instance, in his 1919 Lyman Beecher lectures, Albert Parker Fitch addressed the problem. The way in which he named the issue is worth quoting at length:

> No one, whether learned or pious, or both, is equipped for the pulpit without the addition of that intuitive discernment, that quick and varied appreciation, that sane and tolerant knowledge of life and the world, which is the reward given to the friends and lovers of humankind. For the preacher deals not with the shallows but the depths of life. . . . To make real sermons preach-

---

1. For a similar perspective, see Rachel Held Evans, "Want Millennials Back in the Pews? Stop Trying to Make Church 'Cool,'" in *The Washington Post*, April 30, 2015, www.washingtonpost.com/opinions/jesus-doesnt-tweet/2015/04/30/fb07ef1a-ed01 -11e4-8666-a1d756d0218e_story.html.

ers have to look, without dismay or evasion, far into the heart's impenetrable recesses. They must have had some experience with the absolutism of both good and evil. I think preachers who regard sermons on salvation as superfluous have not had much experience with either. They belong to that large world of the intermediates, neither positively good nor bad, who compose the mass of the prosperous and respectable in our genteel civilization. Since they belong to it they cannot lead it. . . .

Preachers must know, then, that evil and suffering are not temporary elements of humanity's evolution, just about to be eliminated by the new reform, the last formula, the fresh panacea. To those who have tasted grief and smelt the fire such easy preaching and such confident solutions are a grave offense. They know that evil is an integral part of our universe; suffering an enduring element of the whole. . . .

So the preacher is never dealing with plain or uncomplicated matters. It is their business to perceive the mystery of iniquity in the saint and to recognize the mystery of godliness in the sinner.[2]

The preacher must deal "not with the shallows but the depths of life . . ."

No preacher ever brought the gospel to bear on the lives of those in the pews in a way that was truly salvific while wearing floaties and standing in the baby pool of life. If our sermons are to be effective in leading toward transformation, we have to put on our secondhand scuba gear with a half-filled oxygen tank carved out of the cross of Jesus Christ and dive down to those places where humanity really dwells and is drowning—where if you come up too quickly trying to escape, you'll get the bends. We must dive down into hospital rooms, the therapist's office, war zones, dysfunctional families, funeral parlors, and the hungry belly of an impoverished child. We must swim through waters polluted with hatred, loneliness, frailty, despair, physical pain, mental illness, fear, and spilled blood. We must sink into the deepest crevice of the ocean, find the foundation of the Wailing Wall where all the prayer notes of all the generations

---

2. Albert Parker Fitch, *Preaching and Paganism* (New Haven: Yale University Press, 1920), 17–18.

are stuffed into the crack, pull them out, and read them aloud in our sermons if those sermons are to bring the gospel of Jesus Christ to bear on the depths of the state of humanity. The distance from the depth of human existence to the shores of God's grace is as far as that from Golgotha to the empty tomb—an eternal, three-day's journey, which preachers are called to recount Sunday after Sunday after Sunday.

Defining the Human Condition

Even though the difficulty with addressing the human condition with depth is not new, there is an added challenge for preachers doing this today that our forebears in the pulpit did not face. One of the reasons preachers today struggle with proclaiming God's good news in relation to the human condition in ways those in 1919 or 1019 or 219 did not is that we are uncomfortable claiming that there is a *human* condition. In a postmodern world, many would argue that claiming something in such universal terms as a condition that affects all of humanity is invalid. As Steven L. Winter puts it, "For many, it has become a postmodern truism that 'the human condition' cannot be represented, described, or explained as just so many facts about the world. According to the now standard (if somewhat overstated) axiom of postmodernism, everything about humanity is socially contingent."[3]

And, indeed, as someone who has struggled with postmodern challenges to Christian proclamation myself, I am reluctant to disagree with Mr. Winter and try to define narrowly a condition experienced by all humans regardless of age, generation, sex, gender, sexual orientation, race, ethnicity, geographic location, culture, economic situation, genetic variances, language system, political system, education, globalization, and so forth.

---

3. Steven L. Winter, "Human Values in a Postmodern World," *Yale Journal of Law & Humanities* 6, no. 2 (1994): 233.

Still, I am not convinced you can be a full-blown postmodernist *and* be a biblical preacher. First, notice that Winter's claim that "everything about humanity is socially contingent" is, after all, a universal claim. Being socially constructed, one could argue, seems to be a fundamental and unavoidable element of the human condition.

Second, while I consider my worldview to be postmodern in orientation, I hold to a *light* postmodernism, if you will. I am postmodern in the sense that I am less interested in debating what is true and more interested in conversing about how we construct meaning and are constructed by meaning. I am less interested in debating which metanarrative is absolute for all and more interested in offering to others a metanarrative that I have chosen as ultimate for me while listening to the metanarratives they have chosen as ultimate for them. Instead of speaking the word of God in a top-down, authoritative fashion, I am more interested in preachers viewing themselves as contributing to the matrix of conversations that comprise the congregation as a whole. Preachers have a privileged voice in these conversations in that they stand in the midst of the gathered assembly each week and contribute a monologue to the conversation, but these contributions from the pulpit are always made in the context of reciprocal listening to others in the congregation (and the world) as they also offer the word of God.[4]

All of this, however, is a light postmodernism, because I would also argue that the cornerstone upon which the church's biblical preaching is built is the assumption that our ancient texts still speak to contemporary existence *because* the underlying structure of human existence is persistent. That is, in spite of hermeneutical moves that need to be made to account for the difference in the ancient world and worldviews and the contemporary world and worldviews, biblical preachers are committed to the idea that the human condition as portrayed in our ancient scriptures is still the condition faced by humanity today, and that the way God in the ancient text

---

4. For my extended argument for a conversational homiletic intended for a postmodern context, see O. Wesley Allen, Jr., *The Homiletic of All Believers: A Conversational Approach* (Louisville: Westminster John Knox, 2005).

addresses this condition and calls us to deal with the condition is the same today.

Theology and science agree that humans are a unique species in the animal world. The criteria we use to divide living creatures into kingdoms, phyla, classes, and species are certainly subjectively determined. But this does not mean the constructs are without merit. Bigger brains and opposable thumbs allow humans to make meaning of and construct the world in ways other animals cannot. Christian theology has explored this human distinction from the rest of the animal world in relation to the biblical claim that the species is made in the *imago Dei* (Gen 1:26).[5] If this claim is held as a central construct of the Christian faith, then also central must be the claim that a shared condition is part of the heritage of our shared uniqueness in creation.

If that is the case, then what does the term *the human condition* mean for light postmodernist, biblical preachers? The label can be used differently in different contexts. It can include all of the wonders (e.g., beauty, joy, and intimacy) as well as the struggles of human nature, existence, and agency. In the context of this book, however, I will use the phrase as a technical term naming the negative sense of the underlying, structural, existential problems inherent in being and living as human beings. This is not meant to be a reductionist move suggesting the complexity and even glory of the human condition should be ignored in the pulpit, but instead is simply a way to get our subject to a manageable scale fitting for the scope of this book. Our working definition for the sake of preaching that addresses the human condition then is as follows:

> The human condition is composed of the threats and damage done to the physical, intellectual, psychological, spiritual, material, and social well-being of human beings individually and human communities collectively.

---

5. For an extended discussion of this issue in relation to a different topic see Emily Askew and O. Wesley Allen, Jr., *Beyond Heterosexism in the Pulpit* (Eugene, OR: Cascade, 2015).

By "threats and damage" instead of simply "damage," I mean to imply that the human condition is structured not only by injury to our well-being but also by our awareness of the constant potential of injury. The human condition is not only brokenness but recognition of this brokenness that in turn leads to more brokenness.

By "the physical, intellectual, psychological, spiritual, material, and social well-being," I simply mean to imply the whole of the human being is threatened and damaged in this condition of being human.[6] All of these aspects of well-being need not be threatened or injured at the same time to be indicative of the human condition. But the fact that they are all lost in death shows that they are integrally related in life. Thus damage done to one aspect of well-being always raises the awareness of the possibility if not the fact of damage done to other elements of our existence.

By "well-being of human beings individually and human communities collectively," I mean to assert that individualistic, communal, and cultural experiences of the pitfalls and trials of being human must be included in the preacher's purview of the human condition. At times in dealing with the human condition, preachers need to address the congregation as a collection of individuals struggling with individual manifestations of the human condition, and at times we need to address structural or systemic manifestations of the human condition and view the congregation as a community or a collective representation of the wider culture.

Finally, we need to pause over the verb used in the definition: threats and damage *done* to human individuals and communities. There are two sides to this "doing." On the one hand, we humans are the *victims* of threats and damage to our well-being, and on the other hand we are the *cause* of threats and damage to the well-being of others.

---

6. On "well-being," see David Kelsey, "On Human Flourishing: A Theocentric Perspective," esp. pp. 2–3, 8–18, accessed at http://faith.yale.edu/sites/default/files /david_kelsey_-_gods_power_and_human_flourishing_0_0.pdf; see also Marjorie Hewitt Suchocki, *The Fall to Violence: Original Sin in Relational Theology* (New York: Continuum, 1995).

So the victim side of the fickle coin of the human condition is that all of us suffer due to moral and natural evil. While we do not all suffer to the same degree, avoidance of suffering is impossible for humans. Suffering is part of the structure of what it means to be human. All of us know physical pain, emotional loss, spiritual angst, and relational distress. Nowhere in the Bible is the relentlessness of suffering given better witness than in the sheer number of psalms that are individual (3, 4, 5, 6, 7, 9–10, 11, 13, 17, 22, 26, 28, 31, 35, 38, 39, 41, 42–43, 51, 54, 55, 56, 57, 59, 61, 64, 69, 70, 71, 77, 86, 88, 102, 109, 120, 130, 139, 140, 141, 142, 143) and communal (12, 44, 60, 74, 79, 80, 83, 85, 89, 90, 94, 123, 126, 129, 137) prayers of lament or complaint. As Jesus asserts in the Sermon on the Mount, God makes the sun shine on both those who are evil and those who are good and makes it rain on both the righteous and the unrighteous (Matt 5:45). All suffer.

The second side of the coin of the human condition, that of human responsibility, is that all of us sin in ways that harm our relationship with God as well as threaten and damage the well-being of others and ourselves. Paul, more consistently than any other biblical writer, shows how sin is not some occasional act that humans mistakenly do. It is part of the very structure of human existence, which we cannot escape and to which we contribute. Paul names sin as a condition that possesses or enslaves humanity:

> I'm made of flesh and blood, and I'm sold as a slave to sin. I don't know what I'm doing, because I don't do what I want to do. Instead, I do the thing that I hate. But if I'm doing the thing that I don't want to do, I'm agreeing that the Law is right. But now I'm not the one doing it anymore. Instead, it's sin that lives in me. I know that good doesn't live in me—that is, in my body. The desire to do good is inside of me, but I can't do it. I don't do the good that I want to do, but I do the evil that I don't want to do. But if I do the very thing that I don't want to do, then I'm not the one doing it anymore. Instead, it is sin that lives in me that is doing it. (Rom 7:14-20)

And as he says earlier in the letter to the Romans, this is not a condition of some humans; it is the condition of *all* humans: "All have sinned and fall short of God's glory" (3:23).

The depth of the threats and damage done to the physical, intellectual, psychological, spiritual, material, and social well-being of human beings individually and human communities collectively and the inescapable character of suffering and sin call preachers to deal with the human condition carefully, consistently, and constantly. Preachers must find ways to deal with the human condition across the span of their preaching ministry.

A Cumulative Approach to Preaching on the Human Condition

Preachers, of course, should not try to deal with the whole of the human condition, including both sin and suffering, in a single sermon. My concern in this book is with shaping the congregation's process of making meaning of and responding to sin and suffering *over time*. One of my pastors and mentors tells a story of preaching his first sermon in his first parish appointment right out of seminary. He decided he was really going to wow the congregation by synthesizing everything he learned in seminary into one sermon. So he preached and he preached and he preached, bringing in theology, Bible, ethics, history. He sat down exhausted after the sermon and looked at his watch . . . and it had only been eight minutes. He realized quickly that as a preacher he had to focus more narrowly and swim more deeply to have enough to say on any given Sunday. And then you add to that next week, and the week after that, and the month after that, and the year after that.

In any single sermon, preachers must resist the temptation to so thoroughly expose the congregation to trials or horrors of the human condition that it overwhelms them to the point that in the time frame of a single sermon they cannot hear any good news proclaimed. Shock and awe is not an effective homiletical approach.

Sermons should relieve us of our nightmares, not cause them. This is why a cumulative approach to the human condition is necessary if it is to be addressed with true depth. Repeatedly tapping the congregation on the shoulder to point out the situation of our existence will hold more potential for us being raised to the top of that situation than popping the congregation on the nose with a rolled-up newspaper and sending them howling out of the sanctuary.

As Sarah Travis puts it, "[Individual] sermons are always small steps on a much greater journey. Preaching forms and molds congregational identity week by week, idea by idea, text by text."[7] We must preach sin and suffering cumulatively, if we are to have something to say that will help congregations truly experience the relevance of the gospel through proclamation for their particular contexts. We all desire to preach that one sermon that radically changes the lives of those in the pews, but in truth usually the great strength of preaching is seen in terms of more gradual effects.[8] A consciously cumulative approach to one's preaching ministry is a significant means by which a congregation gradually assimilates the vocabulary and grammar of the gospel, shaping individuals as well as the community's understanding and experience of the human condition.

We preachers are trained to focus week after week on certain hermeneutical tasks—exegesis of an ancient text, drawing an analogy between the ancient and the contemporary—and rhetorical elements—sermonic form and imagery as well as delivery—to offer a congregation an "effective" sermonic event. Without detracting from that purpose of preaching, we need to add to these foci an attentiveness to the way this week's sermon builds on what we preached last week and foreshadows what we will say next month and so on and so forth. An analogy I have used elsewhere is that

---

7. Sarah Travis, *Decolonizing Preaching: The Pulpit as Postcolonial Space* (Eugene, OR: Cascade, 2014).

8. In addition to *Homiletic of All Believers* (58–149), I also deal with a cumulative approach to preaching extensively in *Preaching and Reading the Lectionary: A Three-Dimensional Approach to the Liturgical Year* (St. Louis: Chalice, 2007).

preachers must think of themselves as being similar to television scriptwriters when it comes to preaching cumulatively. The scriptwriter must shape an episode of a weekly sitcom or drama to be a single and complete narrative with a beginning, a middle, and an end. Any person tuning into the show for the first time should be able to follow and get something out if it. But the writer must also attend to evolving issues of characterization and subplots that cross over from week to week. The devoted viewer would be aware of and affected by these elements in a way the newcomer would not. When developing and delivering sermons, preachers must attend to both the unique liturgical event of which the sermon is a part so that the sermon stands on its own as well as the cumulative potential the sermon has in intersecting with previous and future sermons.

Again, then, when we think about the human condition in the pulpit, we should be thinking cumulatively. I preach on a small (but deep) element of the human condition this week that adds to a different small (but deep) element I preached on last week and the week before and next week. We cannot, however, simply assume all of these elements will naturally come together in the consciousness of our congregations. If we are not intentional about how these elements fit together, the congregation may experience the different sermons as puzzle pieces that go to different puzzles—they look as though they are related but they actually connect.

Three-Dimensional Model for the Human Condition

I am proposing a three-dimensional schema to help preachers fit together a cumulative approach to preaching on the human condition with the appropriate depth required by both the gospel and the needs of our congregations. While the threats and damage done to human well-being have the two sides of sin and suffering, viewed theologically, they can also be described as having three dimensions that need to be addressed throughout one's preaching ministry.[9] Indeed, each of the three dimensions encompasses both sin and suffering, analogous to the way height has a top and bottom, width has right and left, and depth has front and back.

I propose that we use the greatest commandment as a heuristic lens for approaching the three dimensions of the human condition cumulatively in our preaching: "You must love the Lord your God with all your heart, with all your being, with all your mind, and with all your strength. . . . You will love your neighbor as yourself" (Mark 12:30-31).

While the two commandments deal with an ethic of love expected of us, the language used suggests three different relationships at the center of the human condition.

We start with the command to *love God*. When turned on its head, the command to love God completely—physically, emotionally, and spiritually—intimates that there is a broken relationship between God and humanity. Something is wrong with the vertical dimension of human relationality. The vertical relationship between humanity and God can be said to be broken when, for various reasons, that divine will is not actualized in the world. This brokenness is experienced from the side of human responsibility and from the side of divine responsibility.

The second dimension of the human condition can be viewed through the command to *love your neighbor*. This command intimates that there is a broken relationship between human and human. Something is wrong with the horizontal dimension of human relationality. We have moved, in other words, from the realm of faith and devotion to that of ethics. The horizontal relationship between humanity and humanity can be said to be broken when

---

9. Edward Farley also discusses the human condition in relation to three dimensions, or "spheres," of human reality, but defines them differently than the dimensions described here; they are the interhuman sphere (personal relationships), the social sphere (institutional and social structures) and the personal sphere (individual agency). See *Good and Evil: Interpreting a Human Condition* (Minneapolis: Fortress, 1990), 27–74.

the divine desire for peace, justice, and mercy is not actualized in the world. And this brokenness is experienced from the side of our responsibility for the other (sin) as well as from the side of our victimization by the other (suffering).

The third and final dimension of our heuristic model for the human condition is suggested by the closing phrase of the second command, love your neighbor *as yourself.* When the qualification of loving others *as we love ourselves* is turned on its head, the implication is that the human condition is characterized, in part, by a broken relationship between a person and her or his self. In the metaphor of three dimensions, we are turning to the dimension of depth. What we really mean is that something is wrong with the internal dimension of the human being. The internal relationship between a human and her or his self can be said to broken when, for various reasons, God-gifted meaning of an individual's finite existence is not fulfilled. It is the state of self-estrangement. Because this dimension of the human condition is viewed as a psychological, existential state of being, the two sides of sin and suffering are not simply related in an inseparable fashion as in the previous two dimensions; here they collapse in on one another. Sin against oneself causes and in turn is caused by self-suffering.

In the next three chapters, we will explore each dimension respectively in greater depth. For now, however, I need to clarify a few things about the heuristic model as a whole.

First, every theological school has its own approach to issues related to sin and suffering, a fact that seems to counter the approach of a book making proposals for a cumulative homiletic appropriate across the theological spectrum. For example, there are significant differences in views concerning the cause of sin and suffering. These different views lead to preachers in different theological camps emphasizing one of the three dimensions over the other two. Schools such as evangelicals and the Neoorthodox emphasize brokenness in relation to the vertical dimension. Social gospel and liberation theologians emphasize the horizontal dimension. Pietistic and existentialist theologies emphasize the internal dimension.

Emphasis of one dimension, however, does not mean the other two dimensions are (or should be) ignored in those schools. For the sake of offering a congregation a consistent (systematic) theological outlook, preachers need to be vigilant in interpreting the human condition from the perspective of the emphasis of their theological orientation as the starting point for theological anthropology and name the other two dimensions as *deriving* from the primal dimension. An oversimplified schema of such theological derivation looks like this:

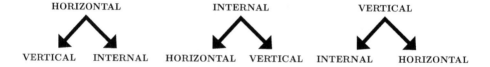

HORIZONTAL   INTERNAL   VERTICAL

VERTICAL   INTERNAL   HORIZONTAL   VERTICAL   INTERNAL   HORIZONTAL

For some, the broken relationship between humanity and God is seen as resulting in the brokenness in human relationships and internal brokenness. For others structural sin at the societal level of human relationship is the cause of brokenness in relation to God and self. And for still others, an internal flawed human character leads to broken relationships with God and others. In all of these perspectives, all three dimensions are crucial to understanding the full depth of the human condition.

Second, in this book, I am trying, as much as is possible, not to force my own particular theology upon the reader. While I am arguing for a particular theological schema, I am not attempting constructive theology. I obviously make a theological argument, but I am not arguing for a particular theological school. I am writing as a homiletician concerned with assisting preachers—all preachers across the theological spectrum—in bringing greater depth concerning the human condition into their preaching ministry. In other words, my hope is that the model I propose can be helpful to any preacher reading this book whether she is an evangelical, existentialist, postliberal, or liberation theologian; whether he is a Presbyterian, Roman Catholic, United Methodist, Pentecostal, Baptist, or Mennonite.

That said, it is appropriate to name my own theological location, since against my will my subjectivity will surely show through to the reader. I was raised in the deep South where my faith was formed in a United Methodist church. The church was a mainline congregation, but, by being in the middle of the Bible Belt, the pietistic strain of Wesleyan theology had a strong evangelical orientation. When I went to college I was introduced to and greatly influenced by the theological trinity of the middle of the twentieth century—Karl Barth, Rudolf Bultmann, and Paul Tillich. I was intrigued with Barth's theological method, clarity, and certainty, but I was claimed by the existentialism of Bultmann's demythologizing program and Tillich's approach to critical correlation. In seminary, however, I was introduced to and influenced by feminist theology narrowly and liberation theologies more broadly and continue to learn from postcolonial theologies and hermeneutics.

Thus I started my theological journey with the vertical dimension as the primary dimension for understanding the human condition. In college it shifted to the inner dimension. And in seminary it never quite shifted to the point that the horizontal was prioritized in my systematic theology, but it rose in importance as a critique over against the individualism I had held to in both of my earlier stages of development, especially the individualism inherent in existentialism. On the leg of my theological journey during which I write this book, I imagine the broken internal relationship as leading to the broken relationship on the horizontal dimension that leads in turn to the broken relationship between humanity and God. But I also see the influence flowing in the reverse direction, in an unending, vicious cycle. I name this on the one hand so that readers can filter out my constructive theological perspective when it seeps through even though I am trying to be descriptive of other perspectives. On the other hand, I name it to help readers start with the simplified descriptions of derivation above and then move to think about the more complex relationship of the dimensions in their own theological system.

In sum, regardless of one's starting point, we must recognize that emphasizing one dimension as the point of origin for sin and suffering over the other two does not diminish the importance of the other two for understanding the full depths of the human condition, but necessitates their inclusion. It is the three dimensions *together* that name the whole of the problem(s) facing the whole of humanity.

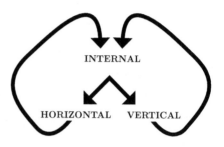

Third, and following from the two points of clarification above, it is important to remember that the three-dimensional model proposed here is artificial. My concern in dividing up the human condition in the way I have is twofold—to provide manageable-sized elements to address in single sermons while offering an overarching way to see how those elements relate in the larger span of one's cumulative preaching ministry. We must not forget in the process of our preaching in this manner, however, that in scripture, tradition, contemporary theology, and experience, the human condition cannot so easily be chunked into different parts.

Take the story of the fall in Genesis 3, which the church has used as a lens through which to understand the human condition. The story has been at times interpreted as the literal cause of the state of humanity and at times as a mythical, theological, or metaphorical description of that state. Regardless of these differences in hermeneutics, all can agree that the story contains all three dimensions in our model. The relationship with God is broken as the humans disobey God and eat from the tree of knowledge of good and evil (vv. 1-6). The relationship between neighbors is broken when the human passes the blame for the act when confronted by God (vv. 8-13). The relationship with self is distorted when the humans recognize their nakedness and experience shame (v. 6). And, finally, while the three dimensions above are described in terms of human responsibility or sin, the story ends with God declaring that humans will suffer even to the point of being kicked out of the garden to face life that ends in death (vv. 16-24). Given the impossibility of disconnecting these three dimensions theologically or experientially, we preachers must remember that we deal with them individually in sermons *in order to* help our congregations experience the gospel as addressing the whole of the human condition cumulatively across the whole of our preaching ministry. Thus we must deal with all three dimensions—that is, both sides of all three dimensions—cumulatively if our hearers are to believe in, trust, and experience the fullness of God's good news.

The Three Dimensions and Scripture

These three dimensions are addressed throughout scripture. Indeed, one could argue that the canon offers a cumulative approach to the human condition. It deals with each dimension in a variety of ways across a spectrum of different biblical works and theological perspectives. Moreover, sometimes biblical texts deal narrowly with suffering or sin in relation to this specific dimension, and at other times they deal with a mixture of dimensions, for instance in how sin against God leads to sin against others and vice versa. The problem is that preachers have been conditioned to look for a much narrower approach to the human condition in the canon.

With the rise of the modern historical consciousness, preachers came to see an essential part of their task as bridging the gap between the ancient world of the Bible and the contemporary world of their hearers. One of the main ways this was done was through an "application" portion of the sermon, usually at the end. The classic Puritan Plain Style of sermon, for instance, moves from exegesis of the ancient text to drawing universal (eternal) theological truths from the text to, finally, applying that truth to the known situation of the hearers. The rise of the modern historical consciousness, however, was accompanied by a rise in confidence in human ability that came from the Renaissance and the Enlightenment. Due to such humanism flooding into the church, the application portion of the sermon came more and more to be a time of exhortation. Application became equated with telling those in the pews what to do.

More conservative theological camps often focused homiletical exhortation in terms of personal morality, while more liberal camps focused on social ethics and those in-between who were influenced by modern psychological sensitivities focused on self-help. The homiletical and hermeneutical dynamic across the spectrum, however, was similar. There are plenty of biblical texts that function in a hortatory fashion and should be preached as such. The problem is that this homiletical approach led preachers to find a basis of exhortation in all texts. Instead of application flowing in whatever direction the exegesis indicated, moral/ethical instruction as a primary homiletical goal overwhelmed exegesis so that it aimed from the beginning toward human action. Thus, in essence, preachers affirmed, consciously or unconsciously, that we humans can address and perhaps even repair the human condition on our own—in God's name to be sure, but on our own.

If as part of our exegesis we attend specifically to the question of what dimension of the human condition the text is dealing, we can curb this tendency. Exhortation will (must!) still have its place, but it will be a more limited place.

Analogies

Texts addressing different dimensions of the human condition (and radically different manifestations of those dimensions) invite different sorts of "applications." Because the word *application* has been limited in homiletical use in the way described above, we should cast it aside for general use. Instead of bridging the gap between the ancient and contemporary in terms of "applying" the text to the hearers, we will do well to draw analogies between the then and the now.

The most thorough work on analogy in preaching is Stephen Farris's *Preaching That Matters: The Bible and Our Lives*.[10] He says, "To 'draw an analogy' is to make a comparison between the similar features or attributes of two otherwise dissimilar things, so that the unknown, or less well known, is clarified by the known."[11] In terms of our topic, I am suggesting that some element of the human condition is what is similar between the ancient text and our contemporary lives and world. What may be dissimilar between the then and the now are the situations in which that element is experienced, the ways the element manifests itself, and the ways the element is named.

Farris suggests that the way to begin finding analogies between the text and our current hearers is to focus on the person or groups in or behind the text with whom contemporary hearers can be invited to identify and consider the ways the contemporary hearers are both unlike and like them.[12]

Take, for example, the story of the hemorrhaging woman in Mark 5:24-34. Even after going to physician after physician, her chronic hemorrhage has persisted for a dozen years. It is unlikely that many in a congregation have experienced this exact physical condition, but some may well be dealing with chronic illness and repeated doctor's visits. But still this is a narrow reading of the woman's condition in terms of looking at the underlying structure of the element of the human condition her particular characterization represents and which *all* of our hearers share. The woman's illness would also make her unclean and thus unable to participate

---

10. Stephen Farris, *Preaching That Matters: The Bible and Our Lives* (Louisville: Westminster John Knox, 1998).

11. Ibid., 8.

12. Ibid., 75–93.

in much of the religious life of the community. Mark presents her as having reached such a point of desperation that she is willing to cross the boundaries of propriety to try to get something from Jesus that she needs to raise up her state of well-being. The fact that the woman can only be healed by supernatural means combined with the exclusion from religious community relates to both the vertical and the horizontal dimensions of the human condition.

This description of the deeper structure of the woman's situation clearly has similarities to something we all experience at different times in our lives. Our hearers know of long-term struggles that have damaged their well-being. Many (all?) know what it is like to be excluded from some community based on something that is completely outside their control. This deeper structure is the point from which homiletical analogies must grow if our sermons are really going to bring the good news to bear on human existence in an effective manner. In looking for points of identification with people in or behind the text, then, the preacher must look below surface-level descriptions to the situations and structures of behavior of the people.

Going below the surface, however, does not justify eisegesis. We should not add details to the text to sharpen a view of the element of the human condition addressed by it. Perhaps the primary way we preachers do this is to psychologize the text. Specifically, we assume to know the emotions of people in or behind the text, when the text gives us no such indication. Above I described the woman with the hemorrhage as having reached a point of desperation. This is a description of her situation that grows out of the narrator's description of her having suffered for twelve years, endured much from physicians, spent all she had, and yet her condition grew worse (vv. 25-26). I did not describe how she *felt* about this desperate situation. When I imagine how she must have felt, I am really imagining how I would feel in similar circumstances. Had I described her as depressed and miserable, I would rule out the possibility of her feeling courageous and hopeful in her struggles. Focus on possible emotional responses to a situation will detract the congregation's attention from the situation itself. They will focus on how the woman supposedly felt and times when they have or have not felt that way, at which point the analogy between the deep structures of the element of the human condition in the situation in or behind the text and the same structures in different contemporary situations will be lost.

Language and Imagery

In the same way that preachers must dig below the surface of characterization in the biblical text to get to the element(s) of the human condition being addressed in a text, we cannot allow ourselves to become comfortable naming and imaging analogous manifestations of the element of the human condition in our own time, lives, and world in shallow ways. Indeed, when we name or show some element of the human condition in our sermons, we should expect some level of discomfort on the part of both us and our hearers.

We must name whatever element of the human condition we are addressing in a sermon with honesty, with clarity, and without blinking. For instance, consider how often in funerals preachers avoid naming that the person lying in the casket in front of the congregation is dead. The very limit of the human condition shared by every human being and with every living creature is denied at the point when it is most undeniable. Funeral preachers use euphemisms, referring to death as being asleep, carried away by the angels, departed, with God, called home. Such resting and journey metaphors may name core beliefs for the pastor and/or the congregation, but they are also part of the human inclination to deny the brutal reality of death lying right in front of the altar. We might as well take Good Friday out of the liturgical year and jump straight from the Mount of Transfiguration to the empty tomb. "Cory died just like we all will die. 'Ashes to ashes; dust to dust.' 'All flesh is grass; all its loyalty is like the flowers of the field.

The grass dries up and the flower withers when the Lord's breath blows on it. Surely the people are grass'" (Isa 40:6-7). This sort of empathetic honesty is what needs to be said to help congregants uncomfortably face the human condition and then to hear a comforting word of resurrecting good news that refuses to allow even the final expression of the human condition to be the final word about the human condition.

Naming the human condition directly without flinching is only part of what we must do as preachers. All good sermons show as well as tell. We must provide imagery that will help our congregations *see* with their ears and imaginations the human condition in which they reside and participate. We too often, however, use sermon illustrations that function in the same way as euphemisms—we picture the element of the human condition being explored with imagery that allows the hearers to not look too closely. We use what a friend of mine likes to call cookie jar images. The preacher names the depth of sin that has us trapped in accordance with Romans 7:19—"I don't do the good that I want to do, but I do the evil that I don't want to do"—and then illustrates it with a three-year-old taking a cookie from the kitchen even though her parent told her not to. All the listeners smile and say, "Aww."

David Buttrick offers three criteria for judging the appropriateness of an image for a sermon: "(1) There must be a clear analogy between an idea in sermon content and some aspect of the illustration; (2) There ought to be a parallel between the structure of content and the shape of an illustration; (3) The illustration should be 'apropriate' to the content."[13]

If we apply these criteria to the cookie jar image, we might find that the first two criteria are met, but the third is not. A Norman Rockwell picture of a sweet but mischievous child sneaking a cookie is not appropriately serious to name the level of entrapment we experience as humans in relation to our inability to avoid sinning. The

---

13. David Buttrick, *Homiletic: Moves and Structures* (Philadelphia: Fortress, 1987), 133.

cookie jar image stays too far away from the real harm that sin does to our well-being.

A little distance in imagery, however, is not necessarily a bad thing—it allows hearers to let down their guard.[14] Before they can look in the mirror, they may need to be shown an image that is detached from the seriousness of their own contribution to and imprisonment in the human condition. But such cutesy, cookie jar images can at best only be starting points for leading the congregation deeper into a consideration of the element of the human condition being shown. Preachers need to offer their hearers mirrors that reflect their lives and their world with the guilt and pain they know (but try to deny) are inherent parts of reality.

These mirrors, of course, need to be held up to the congregation with empathy. We preachers are as embroiled in whatever element of the human condition is under consideration as is the worst scoundrel in the back pew of the balcony. Imagery that is inclusive of the preacher allows us to offer a mirror that reveals guilt and pain instead of evoking shame. When the congregation does not feel judged by the preacher but mired in the same condition as the preacher when shown to them in imagery filled with gravitas, they will be able to let down their guard and consider and experience the imagery with the seriousness the subject matter deserves. If the imagery is not true to life (which would include an image that excludes the preacher), it will not help the congregation hear the fullness of the good news. The gospel, like the cutesy images, will remain at a distance from the hearers.

Bad News to Good News

That last claim bears further unpacking. Preachers do not preach the human condition. That is not our goal. We preach the gospel *in*

---

14. See Michael Brothers, *Distance in Preaching: Room to Speak, Space to Listen* (Grand Rapids: Eerdmans, 2014) for an excellent exploration of types of distance that have been and can be employed in sermons.

light of the human condition. So really, this book focuses on the first half of sermons, if you will—the setup, the bad news that cries out for the louder, stronger, final good news.

This is not meant to imply that every sermon needs to follow a law-gospel structure, but I do think we could do with a little more of it. Paul Scott Wilson has perhaps been the strongest contemporary homiletical voice arguing for this sort of structure with his four-page model for sermons in which the sermon moves from trouble in the ancient text and analogous trouble in the contemporary world to the good news/grace in the text and an analogous expression of such good news/grace in the contemporary world.[15]

A different approach to this sort of logic comes from Eugene Lowry. His narrative approach of the early 1980s was meant to counter traditional propositional kinds of preaching. In doing so he argues for a narrative movement in which sermons flow from an itch to a scratch.[16] Lowry speaks about creating ambiguity and tension for the hearers and taking them deeper into that so that they desire resolution. Itch and scratch are more helpful terms for the preacher than Wilson's trouble and grace because they speak of the *experience* the preacher is trying to offer in the different movement of the sermon instead of just the content being conveyed. In terms of our current focus, then, Lowry argues that hearers need to be made to itch concerning some element of the human condition before they can find relief in a scratch the preacher wants to provide.

This book is intended to help preachers better diagnose and name the *accumulation* of itches that pain humanity so that they can also better proclaim the good news of Jesus Christ that addresses those itches. We preachers do not want the itch in any single sermon to be at the level of the whole body being covered by a hor-

---

15. Paul Scott Wilson, *The Four Pages of the Sermon: A Guide to Biblical Preaching* (Nashville: Abingdon, 1999). For use of imagery related to the human condition that relates to Wilson's "trouble," see Scott Hoezee, *Actuality: Real Life Stories for Sermons That Matter*, The Artistry of Preaching Series (Nashville: Abingdon, 2014).

16. Eugene L. Lowry, *The Homiletical Plot: The Sermon as Narrative Art Form*, expanded ed. (Louisville: Westminster John Knox Press, 2000), 15–21.

rific case of shingles, but neither do we want a single, little bitty mosquito bite that we cure on our own with a little Calamine lotion applied during a commercial break in *Oprah*. A good, solid itchiness caused by the foibles and dangers of humanity *to set up* a word of depth concerning God's grace and calling on our lives and the world—that is what we need in a sermon. And we need it over and over again in relation to the different dimensions of the human condition. We create sermonic itches in relation to the vertical dimension of the human condition *in order to* declare that God is *pro nobis* (for us) and reconciles us to God's self in Christ Jesus. We create sermonic itches in relation to the horizontal dimension of the human condition *in order to* declare that God liberates us from both injuring others and being injured by others. And we create sermonic itches in relation to the internal dimension of the human condition *in order to* declare that in our finite, mortal, flawed lives, God offers us fulfillment in sharing in God's eternal being.

In sum, then, this book attempts to offer a suggestive model for doing a better job of bringing the different dimensions of threats and damage to the well-being of individuals and communities into our preaching over time so that we can do a better job of offering a myriad of perspectives on the good news of salvation and baptismal vocation to those who need saving and long for direction and meaning in their all-too-real human lives.

In aiming for this goal, each of the three dimensions introduced above will be the focus of its own chapter. In each chapter, I will begin by naming the dimension theologically and existentially, unpacking both sides of sin and suffering of the dimension. This descriptive theological task will be followed by a prescriptive one—offering homiletical strategies for dealing with that dimension in the pulpit effectively. This will include an examination of the types of biblical passages that most clearly address the dimensions, discussion of approaches to drawing analogies between ancient views of the dimension and contemporary experiences, suggestions for language and imagery that can be used in helping the congregation see and experience this dimension of the human condition, and possibilities for sermon structures that can be used in moving from the bad news of the dimensions to the good news of God's saving and guiding grace. And finally each chapter will include sermons as case studies for dealing with the dimension under consideration.

The three chapters that follow are intentionally not written to build upon one another in order so as not to presume a theological ordering of the three dimensions. I suggest that readers begin with the chapter that focuses on the dimension of the human condition they view as the theological starting point for thinking about sin and suffering based on their theological orientation and then move to the other two as derivative of that dimension.

THE VERTICAL DIMENSION OF THE HUMAN CONDITION

Our overarching concern in this book is with the preacher's task of proclaiming how God's good news addresses the human condition, that is, how the preacher names and deals with the threats and damage done to the physical, intellectual, psychological, spiritual, material, and social well-being of human beings individually and human communities collectively. We are using the greatest commandment—"You must love the Lord your God with all your heart, with all your being, with all your mind, and with all your strength. . . . You will love your neighbor as yourself" (Mark 12:30-31)—as a heuristic lens through which to view and bring the three dimensions of the human condition into a cumulative homiletical approach.

In this chapter, we are focusing specifically on the vertical dimension of the human condition implied in the command to love God. The very fact that humanity must be commanded to love God wholly implies that we do not do so. There is brokenness in the relationship between God and humanity that threatens and damages our well-being. The implication of the greatest commandment is that we humans are responsible for this brokenness. And such is the case. There is, however, another side to the experience of this brokenness not implied by the commandment but found elsewhere in scripture—that of divine responsibility for human suffering. This vertical dimension of our model of the human condition focuses on personal morality and devotion amongst individuals and human communities along with questions of theodicy, and we will examine both sin and suffering in relation to them.

Brokenness in the relationship between God and humanity is the usual starting point for dealing with the human condition by theologians and preachers who reject anthropology as an appropriate starting point for doing theology—for example, some in fundamentalist, evangelical, Roman Catholic, Neoorthodox, Reformed, and postliberal schools of thought. There is a good rationale behind this emphasis. This dimension is the one most often and most explicitly named in scripture and has been the one receiving the most attention in orthodox theology throughout the history of the church. For preachers who hold the vertical dimension as primary for understanding the human condition, the horizontal and inner dimensions are seen as derivative of the vertical. In other words, if the core problem of the human condition is seen as brokenness in the relationship between humanity and God, then this brokenness in turn causes brokenness in relationships with our neighbors and in the relationship of a person with him- or herself.

Conversely, for those who hold that either of the other two dimensions are primary for understanding the human condition theologically, the vertical dimension is seen as resulting from either brokenness in human relationships or an inner brokenness. Regardless of where one starts, however, any description of the human condition or cumulative preaching that fails to deal adequately with sin and suffering related to humanity's relationship with God offers only a partial and thus a flawed understanding of the situation in which we humans exist.

Of course, theologians and preachers cannot be reduced to similarities in all the ways they approach this vertical dimension of the human condition. For example, different thinkers approach the very purpose of theology and the way theological language functions in different ways. Some assume theological language works as a literal description of God and the human condition, while others argue that theological language functions across a spectrum of metaphorical, symbolic, and literal descriptions. Preachers from different theological orientations, therefore, have different roles, ranging from simply repeating and expounding the way traditional theological language names the human condition and God's response to it, to interpreting, translating, and updating that language in ways that are meaningful to contemporary hearers.

Still, in one way or another, scholars and preachers dealing with this dimension of the human condition emphasize the sovereignty of God. God is the transcendent Other, almighty creator of and provider for the world, who must and does reveal God's self to the world so that we can know God as *pro nobis* ("for us"). While different thinkers and schools name the way God exercises this divine sovereignty differently, they agree that God is in some way responsible for and has dominion over the world and human history. As Alpha and Omega, God not only brought the world into being but has a purpose (*telos*) for the world and for us humans who inhabit it that involves us being in right relationship with God. Thus God's providential care for humanity stretches from creation to eschaton.

Expressed conversely from the human side, theology focusing on the vertical dimension recognizes that humans are utterly dependent upon God. This dependence need not imply that humans have no freedom, but it does mean that our existence, survival, salvation, vocation, and freedom—that is, our well-being—all come from God. This assertion is not simply a call for a way to view the world, but a statement about the way the world is whether we acknowledge it or not.

In other words, everything that humans do is in response to God's initiative, whether we recognize it or not. God creates and everything else follows. God calls us to respond, individually and corporately, with complete trust in and grateful recognition of God's care for us and with obedience to God's will.

Sin

Theological

We fail miserably in responding with such trust, gratitude, and obedience, however. This dimension of the human condition is expressed in terms of humans rebelling against the very structure of our dependent existence. We do not love God with our whole heart, soul, strength, and mind. We sin against God "in thought, word, and deed, by what we have done and by what we have left undone" (BCP).

We fail to trust, indeed are unable to trust, in God even though we are utterly dependent upon God. The result, then, is that we place our trust elsewhere. We have a wide range of sinful actions against God, but structurally speaking, all acts of disobedience and rebellion are really expressions of idolatry. The Decalogue opens with four commandments that all deal with this fact. The Israelites were commanded to have no other gods before Adonai, make and worship no idols, make no wrongful use of Adonai's name, and observe the Sabbath (Exod 20:1-11). To break any of these commandments is to place something else before God. The fact of the matter is, however, that no matter how well intentioned we are when we say, "As for me and my household, we will serve the Lord" (Josh 24:15), we fail over and over again and are unable to succeed in our willingness and ability to trust in God and God's will for us. We, knowingly and unknowingly, serve and worship something else as a means of self-service and self-worship. The sovereign God cannot not be molded into Santa Claus or a good-luck charm. Thus we turn, over and over again, to golden calves, patriotism, family ties, money, privilege, position, and the likes because these gods can be made to serve us. As Paul says, "The desire to do good is inside of me, but I can't do it. I don't do the good that I want to do, but I do the evil that I don't want to do" (Rom 7:18-19).

Our failure in our vertical relationship with God, however, is not the last word on this dimension of the human condition. Our sinful nature is answered by God's character. Our worship of lesser gods (including ourselves) is countered by the one, true God. Because God is just and righteous in God's will for humanity, God judges our iniquity. But God does not forget our utter dependence on God even when we do. God remains *pro nobis* even when we turn against God. God remembers God's covenants with us. God brings us to repentance. God forgives our sin. And God reconciles us to God's self. *This* is the last word on the vertical dimension of the human condition. But such good news can only be proclaimed, heard, and experienced if word of our sinfulness is named first.

Biblical

Throughout Israel's history as told and interpreted by the various writers in the Hebrew Bible, human sinfulness is portrayed in Technicolor fashion. Adam and Eve disobey God's direct order. The people try to build a tower to the heavens to make a name for themselves. After God rescues the slaves from Egypt, they fashion a golden calf in the wilderness. Over and over again, the Israelites turn to foreign gods such as Ba'al. Individuals, tribes, priests, and kings are all indicted.

Yet God's *hesed* (steadfast loving-kindness) is continually extended to the people even though they turn away from God. We turn from God, and God establishes covenants with the people through Noah, Abraham and Sarah, Moses, and David, and reestablishes and reaffirms this covenantal relationship through the prophets. Even when our disobedience pushes God to announce, "You are not my people, and I am not your God" (Hos 1:9), God does so in order that God can restore the relationship and reclaim us as God's people ("In the place where it was said to them, 'You are not my people,' it will be said to them, 'Children of the living God'" [v. 10]). God judges *so that* God might forgive. And forgive God does, over and over again, reconciling the idolatrous and self-serving to God's self.

The New Testament likewise portrays our sinfulness and God's rescue in relation to the vertical dimension. The Christ event can be interpreted through the lens of the vertical dimension of the human condition as an expression of God's reconciliation of us to God's self. Substitutionary and satisfaction views of the atonement that grow out of New Testament metaphors for salvation are attempts to describe how humanity has broken our relationship with God through idolatrous disobedience and rebellion and has become an offense to God's righteousness . . . yet, God's will to be reconciled to us is greater than our condition of sinfulness. Through Christ's birth, ministry, crucifixion (especially the crucifixion!), and resurrection, God atones us—makes us "at one" with God. Through the faithfulness of the one who ate with tax collectors and sinners, we are justified while we are yet guilty. Even though we are unable to be in right relationship with God, God proclaims through the Christ event that God is in right relationship with us. Salvation experienced in terms of being put in right relation with God thus results in well-being in terms both of this earthly existence and eternal life.

Homiletical

It is a difficult task for preachers to convince their congregations that they are idolaters. Oh, it is easy to find examples of our idolatry to use in sermons. It is simply hard for us to recognize or admit that such examples are really idolatrous.

I continue to find Paul Tillich's classic description of idolatry useful for helping people today intellectually grasp that people (maybe not themselves) are idolatrous as surely as if they sacrificed their best calf at an altar stationed before a bronze statue.[1] Tillich

---

1. Paul Tillich, *The Dynamics of Faith* (New York: Harper, 1957).

argues that all humans have a hierarchy of concerns. We value our car more than our bicycle, our home more than our car, and our family more than our home. Not only is there nothing wrong with such a hierarchy, it is a perfectly normal and healthy way of shaping our priorities. Yet something must be (and always is) at the top of the hierarchy of our concerns. There is something that I hold more valuable than everything else. There is something that concerns me more than anything else concerns me. Understood in this way, Tillich can say that there is no such thing as an atheist, because everyone has an ultimate concern, everyone has a god she or he worships and serves. Conversely, it could be argued that there is no such thing as a person who is not an idolater, because we all place other concerns above our concern for God, at least from time to time.

While Tillich's description of ultimate concern (when used repeatedly in the pulpit) can help a congregation understand idolatry in the abstract, we must admit that there is a difference between understanding the issue in our heads and recognizing it in our hearts when it is staring us back in the mirror. We can understand the "dynamic" of idolatry, see it practiced by others, and yet be oblivious to our own captivity by it. We humans have an amazing ability to deny the very conditions that damage our well-being.

Let us consider two examples that many would argue are the most thoroughgoing forms of idolatry in the corporate church—indeed, even in the pulpit—in the United States today and which are nevertheless nigh impossible to get the church to admit, face, and deal with.

The first is *materialism or consumerism*. Humans must, of course, own and consume things to survive. Expressed from the opposite side, it can be argued that lack of economic and social ability to own and consume at levels above the poverty line do damage to human well-being. Food, clothing, and shelter are necessary for existence. To thrive, however, humans need to be able also to consume possessions and services that offer us joy and beauty. If the world is created by God, then owning and using items and services that grow out of creation and human manipulation of created things can be good.

The problem, however, is that as a culture our need for "things" has been subsumed by our desire for more things, which has in turn been subsumed by our obsession for more and more things. There has been a societal shift from consumption as a human practice to consumerism as an unconscious worldview. As John G. Stackhouse defines it, consumerism is "an outlook, a way of seeing things, a way of responding to the world, that frames everything in terms of consumption by oneself."[2] Stackhouse goes on to name the main tenets of a consumeristic worldview:

1. The self is both judge of what is good and the primary beneficiary of what is good.

2. What is good is what the market (of individual consumers) says is good.

3. All else has value only in light of (1) and (2), and therefore properly can be regarded, disregarded, or manipulated in that light.

4. Goods (note the pun) can be bought.[3]

Because it is a self-serving ideology (1 and 2) and everything is evaluated and used in relation to what serves the self (3), and because we do not hold this posture consciously, consumerism is a most vicious form of idolatry. We are not simply talking about greed when we speak of consumerism but a system of evaluating everything, including the self, in relation to a perceived market value.

Consumerism is as prevalent in the church as it is in the rest of North American culture. Let us discuss two interrelated ways it manifests itself. The first way is seen in the phrase "church shopping." Christianity is something to be evaluated and consumed on

---

2. John G. Stackhouse, "Consumerism," in his book *Humble Apologetics: Defending the Faith Today* (New York: Oxford University Press, 2002), 55.

3. Ibid., 56–59.

the same sort of terms that one would buy a couch. There are good reasons to compare and contrast congregations when considering joining one. We should attend and participate in a community of faith whose beliefs and practices promise a certain level of coherence with our devotion to God-in-Christ while challenging us to mature and stretch in our theology and devotion. But most church shopping is less about testing a congregation in relation to one's devotion to God and more about matters of taste. Do I *like* the church? Is the preacher entertaining? Do the facilities include a gym? Do I prefer organ music or guitar and drums?

It is problematic enough when individual Christians approach joining a church on the basis of taste, but the idolatry of consumerism increases when congregations themselves buy into this approach to choosing a church. Evangelism gives way to marketing in the worse sense of the word. One Yellow Pages advertisement for a church is a picture of three different types of cups sitting atop a mound of coffee beans. Above the cups reads "A church where you can CHOOSE YOUR BLEND." Under the cups respectively are the labels "Traditional," "Contemporary," and "Emerging." There are many good reasons for churches embracing various forms of worship, but simply trying to gain a bigger portion of the market by diversifying products for consumption is not one of them. When the church evaluates and shapes its mission in capitalistic terms of success, one can rightly question whether God is the community's ultimate concern.

An even more horrific way that some churches have given in to the idolatry of materialism and consumerism is the proclamation and promotion of some form of the prosperity gospel.[4] When we are awake at 2:00 a.m. because the burdens of life weigh on us so heavily, what do we find on television but a gaggle of used-car salespeople claiming to be preachers who promise a blessing if you will simply buy their clunker. Prosperity theology distorts the biblical

---

4. For a history of the prosperity gospel movement, see Kate Bowler, *Blessed: A History of the American Prosperity Gospel* (New York: Oxford University Press, 2013).

view of God as One who wills to bless us and the Puritan heritage of prosperity as a gift from God instead of something earned solely on the basis of human achievement into a religion that is a step-by-step path to health, wealth, and success.

The promise of blessing is always dependent on the sacrifice of the one seeking the blessing and the benefit received by the one proclaiming the promise. In other words, one of the required steps, and sometimes the only step required by the preacher, is sending money to the ministry or church that is delivering the message. With incredible guile, televangelists fly to a rally in their private jets and wear a suit that costs more than what many in the audience have as equity in their home or saved in their bank account, and then they promise that giving one's last few coins to them will result in a miraculous influx of funds from God.

While this popular religious theme is most blatantly represented in televangelists' preaching, it finds its way into local churches in more subtle, yet very real, ways. Stewardship drives equate doing God's will with giving to the congregational budget, implying (although rarely stating explicitly) that we will be rewarded for obeying God. Similarly, there is often found a self-help, therapeutic approach to the faith that follows the same logic of the prosperity gospel even if it does not focus on money or on the miraculous. The logic is that by properly applying certain spiritual/religious techniques one can improve the state of one's life really without regard to any external referent to the Divine. Even if the focus is not specifically on money or possessions, the approach is consumeristic. By consuming this approach to faith, we raise the value of and satisfaction in our lives. No wonder Dr. Phil and T. D. Jakes are allies.

The second form of idolatry that especially challenges the church (and the pulpit) today is nationalism. No more evidence of a worship of nation is needed than the presence of the American flag in Christian sanctuaries across the land and across the theological spectrum. Often larger than the cross and standing right next to the pulpit are the stars and stripes in all its old glory.

I once drove by a church with a flag pole right by the church sign. At the top of the pole was the American flag. Beneath it was the Christian flag. On the sign read the words "No man can serve two masters." Clearly the church had no clue that the very scripture they were quoting was an indictment of their own idolatry.

It is not, of course, sinful—or even wrong—to love one's country. Evolutionary processes have rendered humans pack animals. We survive by binding together and organizing into mutually supportive groups—friendships, families, clans, cultures, and countries. Part of naming who we are is to distinguish "us" from "them." There are good historical, social, political, and economic reasons for creating such boundaries around us and ours.

The problem is when our love for "us" becomes a higher concern than our love for God, often evidenced by the fact that we assume the two are the same. If we claim to be children of God, then we are citizens of God's creation and God's reign first and only subsequently citizens of our particular nation, state, tribe, region, and so on.

It is easy for us to point out when patriotism becomes sinful in the case of others. While we love to cite Nazism as religion and nationalism combined in a way that the former served the latter in the most horrid of ways, it is incredibly difficult for the church in the United States to confess our own idolatry in this vein. Yet in recent years an exchange student from Germany was living in the States and, given his own sense of history, was shocked to find the American flag and the Christian flag on either side of the cross in the church he was visiting. He said it reminded him of Jesus being crucified between the two thieves.

Of course, the church's nationalistic idolatry is not evidenced only in the display of the flag. We also celebrate national holidays in ways similar to the celebrations of liturgical holy days throughout the church year. As a pastor, I had church members dislike my decision that we not sing Christmas carols during Advent, but they absolutely revolted when I refused to allow the choir to sing a "patriotic cantata" on the Sunday before the Fourth of July. Years later, I attended a church that was a typical, staid, Euro-American congregation. Emotions were internalized and rarely exhibited in worship. The only time applause was offered was when the children's choir sang once a quarter, and it was polite, gentle applause. But on the Sunday before Veterans Day, the choir sang the fight song for each branch of the military while the pastor yelled out—yes, yelled like a cheerleader—for the veterans of that branch to stand, and the congregation erupted in applause and vocal expressions reminiscent of the student section in an SEC football stadium. The gospel reading later in the service received no response whatsoever. I would not be surprised to learn that on that day Jesus wept once again in grief over the death of a friend.

Civil religion and consumeristic religion are by no means the only forms of idolatry facing individual Christians and communities of faith today, but they are prominent and troubling examples of such idolatry. Dealing with these in the pulpit will lead our congregations to deal with all the forms of idolatry that tempt and entrap them.

First, we preachers must admit our own participation in the church's consumeristic and nationalistic idolatry. Some of us have committed the sin of being priests in this idol worship, and others have committed sins of omission in the sense of failing to be prophets naming the idolatry. I refused to allow the Independence Day music program move ahead in worship, but I compromised and allowed it to be offered as a program at the Wednesday evening potluck—which had higher attendance than Sunday worship. And I never succeeded in getting the American flag removed permanently from any church I pastored.

Second, we must name these idolatries of our hearers with empathy. Our people, like us, do need to repent of these sins and strive to put all other concerns in their proper position below our devotion to God. But they, like us, will fail. We know the good, but we cannot do it. Like the Israelites in the wilderness, we turn to golden calves out of fear, not conscious theological reasoning. And our fearful failure results in damage to our own well-being. God may be a jealous God but is not made less-than-God by our idolatry. We, on the other hand, are made less—much less—than we are when we place something unworthy at the pinnacle of our life and loyalties. Similar to the saying, "You are what you eat," we could say, "We are what we worship." When we lift up to the level of ultimate concern something like consumption, then the meaning of our lives is lowered to that which we consume. To address idolatry in the pulpit is to offer a diagnosis that leads to healing. Thus we show our hearers their idolatry not to condemn them but that they might experience God's act of reconciling idolaters to God's self.

Third, for our hearers to be able to see and confess their own idolatry, we must not just slap it up on the projection screen or mirror. We must *show* them idolatry instead of only *telling* them about it, but we can ease them into looking at themselves by creating some distance for them in examining idolatry. Preachers can begin with small idolatrous foibles at which people can laugh a little—"We love our basketball team so much around here we have to set the church calendar around the season schedule"—and build to more and more serious examples—"We have come to see Christmas so much as a holiday focused on exchanging gifts instead of the Nativity that some churches cancel worship services when Christmas falls on a Sunday." Or we can show others' idolatry—"Have you ever paid attention to the way televangelists are always asking for money?"—as a way of introducing our own—"Our stewardship drives may not take advantage of people in that way, but we do push for money, don't we?"

Fourth, we should evaluate each sermon dealing with the vertical dimension of the human condition in relation to other sermons dealing with the same dimension. We need not try to deal with idolatry once and for all in any single sermon. Brokenness in our relationship with God is a chronic condition. It is not going away. We must come at it over and over again to impact our people in a lasting way. That means we can and should deal with small aspects of our sinfulness toward God in individual sermons—just enough to hang in the ear for a while—in a way that foreshadows more expansive understandings and experiences of the issue.

We need sermons that are simple (that is, tightly focused) but that are not simplistic (that is, shallow). The sermon must deal with an aspect of the vertical dimension that is deep enough to engage the hearers existentially, but narrow enough that they are able to hear good news in relation to the bad news. And the mention of good news raises the final suggestion for preaching on sin in relation to the vertical dimension: the punchline of the sermon should be proclamation of God's good news, of God as *pro nobis*. This good news must be larger than the description of the sin. To be so it must be proclamation, not exhortation. Telling people to quit being idolatrous is not good news. Showing them ways God overcomes our idolatry is.

Sample Sermon

The following sermon was preached as part of commencement exercises at Lexington Theological Seminary. The text for the sermon is 2 Samuel 6:1-15, an odd story in which Uzzah is struck down by God when he reached out to keep the ark of the covenant from falling off the cart as it was being taken to Jerusalem. During seminary, students focus so much on their vocation, they can develop an idolatry of their ministry. As the students are leaving school, they are filled with both high expectations and great fear concerning the work of the pastorate. This sermon aims at helping them put their work in proper perspective by recalling the sovereignty of God in relation to that work.

C'mon, admit it. When you woke up this morning, you said to yourself, "Today at Graduates' Communion, I really hope Dr. Allen preaches on that story about David bringing the ark of the covenant to Jerusalem. That would make the perfect graduation gift!"

You said to yourself, "Dr. Allen, please don't preach on something like the Great Commission: What has that text got to do with going off from seminary into ministry in a post-Christian age? Please don't preach on the image of the church in Acts, or Paul's talk about gifts of the Spirit, or the Pastorals' advice to those who would be church leaders. What do those have to say to use about what the church needs from us?"

You said, "Wes (you referred to me as Wes because you don't have to take any more of my classes or receive any more grades from me), don't preach on one of those call stories of the prophets. What have they got to do with the need for the church to speak truth to power in today's society? Moreover, if I have to sing 'Here I Am, Lord,' at LTS one more time, I may run away before I even get my diploma and go to some other school and get an MBA."

Admit it, at that point you fell to your knees and prayed, "Almighty God in heaven, send your Holy Ghost on Wes and lead him to preach on the story of Uzzah being struck down dead for touching the ark of the covenant, because it's my favorite scripture passage about ministry."

Well, God listened. I listened . . . and I have responded faithfully. . . . But for the life of me I can't figure out why you wanted this passage. I can't figure out what image of ministry you see in this story. In fact, when I first read this scene I was . . . well, a little disturbed at the way it portrays the ark of the covenant, since the ark represents God.

You remember the ark of the covenant from your Hebrew Bible courses, don't you? Okay, that's asking too much: Do you remember it from the Indiana Jones movie? Historians don't know a lot about it. It seems to have basically been a box. But what a box! It may have contained some fetish, such as a rock that came from

Mt. Sinai or that was considered to be part of the original tablets of the Ten Commandments.

But it was also considered to be God's throne . . . or God's footstool. The ancient Israelites imagined that the invisible God was sitting on the ark or sitting on a throne above it with God's feet resting on it. Either way, before the temple was built, the ark was considered to signal the actual presence of God. Whatever it was, wherever it was, there was God.

Now it's not so much the ancient belief that God is located around a box that disturbs me. While I certainly don't accept the ancient belief that God is localized, the view is easy to understand in its historical context. What it is about the story that makes me wonder why you would want me to preach on it is that part about God zapping Uzzah for trying to be a good guy. It would seem that the road to hell really is paved with good intentions. Let me remind you what happened—you know, the whole bigger story.

Since they thought God was actually present in or on the ark, the Israelites treated it as a totem and carried it with them to bring them success and protection. They would carry it into battle, assuming that if God were with them, there was no way their enemies could prevail against them.

Well, back before Israel had a king and even before Samuel was high priest, the twelve tribes were at war with the Philistines. After losing a battle, they brought the ark to the battlefield so that they could assure a victory on the following day; but they were wrong about the ark. God can't be molded to our will the way a box can be carried across a field. The Philistines were stronger, won the battle, and captured the ark.

The Philistines took the ark back home to the town of Ashdod as part of the spoils of war. Like the Israelites, they thought by having God there, they would bring blessing to Ashdod; but it only brought them a curse.

The statue of their god, Dagon, literally fell apart in front of the ark, and everyone in the town became covered with tumors. So they put it on a cart pulled by two cows and sent it back to Israel without anyone driving the cart.

It arrived in an Israelite town called Beth-shemesh. At first the people of the town were excited that the ark had been returned to Israel—God had not forsaken them! But the ark brought bad fortune to Beth-shemesh as well, with the result that seventy men of the town were slaughtered.

So Beth-shemesh placed it in the care of the house of Abinadab out on the outskirts of town up on a hill where no one went, so that it wouldn't bother anyone. So that God wouldn't bother anyone. The ark stayed in the care of Abinadab's household throughout the end of Samuel's reign and the whole of Saul's reign over the tribes and into the start of David's reign.

In the ancient world, political power and religious influence were inseparable. When David became king, he set up Jerusalem as his political capital and decided to move the ark there to centralize his rule over the twelve tribes—it was sort of the flip side of our desire to put an American flag in the sanctuary. So David went to a great deal of trouble. He took a platoon of soldiers with him. They placed the ark on a brand-new cart; got two of Abinadab's sons, Ahio and Uzzah, to guide the cart; and David and all his men made music and danced in front of the cart.

It must have been quite a parade. All the kids lined the streets hoping the clowns on the miniature motorbikes would throw them some bubble gum. But the parents came to see the demonstration of the power of their new king and his army, dancing down the road in their dress uniforms with all of their medals jangling on their chest. It was quite a show . . . right up until the cart hit a bump. The oxen pulling the cart stumbled, the cart tipped, and the ark was about to crash to the ground . . .

In the movie *Glory*, the unit of black Union soldiers volunteer to lead the charge against an impenetrable Confederate fort. Just before they are to face the horrific battle, the colonel asks, "If our flag falls, who will pick it up?" The man who had been the worst soldier and biggest whiner in the unit throughout the movie now steps forward and volunteers, "I will."

I could imagine a similar scene taking place before the parade to Jerusalem. David asks, "If the ark tips and starts to fall, who will steady God?" and Uzzah, the short, skinny kid who went into the ministry to avoid the draft, steps forward and says, "I will." And he does.

Now, you'd think God would be pleased with Uzzah's heroic act. Didn't he save the Lord's throne from being scratched, or bent, or burst into pieces beyond the ability of any carpenter's glue to mend it? But for some reason God wasn't pleased. The very opposite: God struck him down because he reached out to rescue the ark.

Underneath the ancient superstition that the ark is a totem of God's presence is an assertion about the nature of God that has a depth of insight to which I rarely aspire. You see, what Uzzah did that evoked God's wrath was to take the presence and power of God for granted. He had become so comfortable with the idea that God was sitting on the ark right there beside him that he felt he could reach out and steady God. Buddy Yahweh needs my help.

Uzzah had lived with the ark at his house his whole life.

- He had studied service to the ark online at ITS, Israelite Theological Seminary, previously known as College of the Torah.
- Graduated with honors and received the Most Likely to Accompany the Ark to Jerusalem Award given by the dean.

- His commission on ministry had approved him with flying colors, and he was ordained at First Christian Church in Kiriath-Jearim.
- Day in and day out he worked faithfully in his ministry:
  - He would preach about the ark, saying how God needs us to serve it.
  - He would mention the ark in prayers at the bedside in the ICU, bringing its comfort to those who were ill.
  - When he would lead the youth group on mission trips to some land ravaged by locusts he would always say, the ark of the Lord of hosts, who is enthroned on the cherubim, has no hands and feet but ours.

He was a faithful servant. But he was unconsciously arrogant in his faithfulness. God is unable to do anything unless we do it for God? Uzzah had become so comfortable with the presence of God that he thought he could steady God, as if the sovereign Creator of the universe and Ruler of the heavens needs a mere mortal minister to steady the Divine One. He led his congregation in singing, "What a friend we have in Elohim," every Sunday, but he had become theologically dyslexic and thought the words were, "What a friend God has in us." He never would have admitted that he believed it, but he had a low arkology—he thought the ark was simply a moral example for Israel, and acted like God's will and work was dependent on him. It was an idolatry that relegated God to being less than God.

I don't know how it is for you, but for me when I have to get up and teach and preach about who God is every week, I begin to convince myself that I really understand, that I really do have a handle on this whole God thing. I forget about the mysterious side of God because I spend so much time concentrating on the minute part of God's nature that I know anything about. It's like spending my whole life with a group of people gathered around me on one side of a solid, wooden fence. I am looking through a small knothole trying to describe to the crowd what I see on the other side. After doing this day in and day out, I forget that I'm looking through a knothole, and I assume that I'm seeing everything there is to see on the other side of the fence. But actually most of what there is to know of God—of God's being, God's grace, God's will, and God's power—lies on the other side of that fence off to the sides of my visual range.

Day after day I live with my knothole's worth of knowledge of God. There's nothing wrong with that, because that's the most we puny, finite beings can ever hope to know of Infinity. What's wrong is when I forget my ignorance and assume that I know God fully—or even fully enough. What's wrong is when I assume that I know God so well that I can just reach out and touch God. How arrogant to think that my knothole view offers me enough of God that I know God needs me to keep God from tipping over! Regardless of what degree we earn, we can never imagine that we have mastered divinity.

Even though I didn't recognize it at first, the way you must have, this odd, troubling story is one of good news. It's an affirmation that God is indeed with us. We so often talk about divine presence in comforting, emotional kinds of ways. Those expressions of God's presence have their place, but this story reminds us that we can never get too touchy-feely with the ark of the covenant. Nor do we need to. Individuals may fail. The church may decline. Nations may fall. The dollar may shrink. Societies may crumble. But by contrast . . . and to put it as straightforward as the text does . . . God is God.

God is sovereign.

- God welcomes our ministry.
- God uses our ministry.
- God does not need our ministry;
  we are in ministry because we need God.
- God accepts our ministry not because God must,
  but as a gift to us.

It's no accident that a key metaphor for faith in the Hebrew Bible is fear of the Lord. Once David gets over his shock and anger at what God did to Uzzah and is reminded of the benefits of serving the ark, he embraces fear of the Lord in a whole new way. No more taking God for granted.

After some initial hesitancy, he does continue bringing the ark the rest of the way to Jerusalem. But this time he dances before the ark in humility—wearing only a loincloth. This time, he stops every six steps and offers a sacrifice to God, before moving another six paces. There is great rejoicing in God's presence tempered with great respect for the power that presence represents. Now that's an image of ministry for the church: when confronted with the incredible power and radical otherness of God, we mere mortal ministers are forced to recognize that we all dance naked before the Lord, no matter how well we dance.

That's why we call what happens tomorrow "commencement" and not "completion." In your program here, we have taken a drill and tried to make the knothole through which you peer at God a little larger. But you're still looking through a knothole trying to catch a glimpse of infinite power, glory, and love. You're still just getting started, so don't get too comfortable in your own gifts and graces. Hopefully, while you have been here you've mastered some skills that will serve you well in your ministry. But you have only begun to develop a pastoral life in which you recognize God as the master of any piddly, little gift we have to offer.

Annie Dillard has a wonderful essay in which she juxtaposes Christian worship with a polar expedition that underestimated the struggles that would be faced in an Arctic adventure. Over and over again, she portrays us bumbling about the task of worship.

- A bad, amateur country-western group leading the sung responses in Catholic Mass

- Communion wafers stuck together and becoming a distraction to the minister
- Inappropriate, self-serving concerns lifted up during the prayers of the people
- Members fussing over being forced to pass the peace to people they don't like
- Something from *The Sound of Music* being played during the offertory

We worship like dancing bears instead of like a dancing king who fears the Lord enough to take off all symbols of his achievements and power and stop every six steps to offer a sacrifice to the Infinite One we describe with finite terms of all-knowing, all-loving, all-powerful.

Dillard says,

> On the whole, I don't find Christians, outside of the catacombs, sufficiently sensible of conditions. Does anyone have the foggiest idea what sort of power we blithely invoke? . . . The churches are children playing on the floor with their chemistry sets, mixing up a batch of TNT to kill a Sunday morning. It's madness to wear ladies' straw hats and velvet hats to worship; we should all be wearing crash helmets. Ushers should issue life preservers and signal flares; they should lash us to our pews.

Our God is a loving and compassionate God. But the God we serve in ministry is also a fiercely mighty God. Crash helmets and life preservers: that's a view of ministry I can believe in. You chose well when you asked for this text as a model to send you off in ministry. Good luck.

Suffering

Theological

Having examined the task of preaching in relation to the broken relationship between God and humanity from the side of human responsibility, we turn now to the other side of the relationship.

What responsibility does God have for brokenness in the vertical dimension of the human condition? In other words, we turn from the category of sin to that of suffering.

Humans suffer in a wide range of ways, individually and corporately. We suffer due to natural causes, the actions of others, and our own actions. When viewed in terms of the vertical dimension of the human condition, however, different forms of suffering share a theological structure in that they all raise the question of theodicy. Pastors know these questions all too well. We are asked them in the hospital when a parent wants to know why God allowed her eighteen-month-old son to have leukemia. We are asked them in Bible studies and discussion groups when Alex says, "Why doesn't God just put a stop to all this [war, poverty, domestic violence, racism, ecological disaster, slavery, patriarchy, and the like]?" We are asked them when people in the church read something like the still-popular *When Bad Things Happen to Good People* by Rabbi Harold S. Kushner.[5] We are asked them when Taylor suggests praying for the victims of the latest hurricane, tornado, earthquake, tsunami, or wildfire during the sharing of prayer concerns in worship but goes on to note that the prayers may be a little too late. We are asked them in the funeral home when a kindhearted but theologically unsophisticated lay member told the bereaved that God loved Mia so much that God wanted her for God's self, and the spouse spats back, "Why does God get her? Why does God's love count for more than mine?" Indeed, the whole of modernity (and postmodernity) cannot escape the question when it was posed with such terrible levels of evil and proficiency in the Holocaust. How could God allow the mass extermination of the Chosen People in the way that modern technology coupled with hatred enabled? Pastors are asked the question of theodicy continually in pastoral situations but address it explicitly in the pulpit far too rarely. That should not be the case if we want our proclamation of God's good news to touch

5. Harold S. Kushner, *When Bad Things Happen to Good People* (New York: Schocken Books, 1981).

the depths of our hearers' existential concerns and the core of their theological worldview.

The word *theodicy* comes from the Greek roots for *God* (*theos*) and *justice* (*dikē*). The question of theodicy, then, deals with the fairness of divine care for the world. God as creator made the world as it is and thus is responsible for the state of the world. God has promised to provide for the world and thus is responsible for its ongoing condition. God is in some way responsible for all that happens in the world. If God is sovereign and thus all-powerful (that is, able to address human suffering), all-knowing (aware of human suffering), and all-loving (desires to address human suffering), then why is there suffering in the world? If God wills the good for us, why is so much of human existence not very good? In other words, from this angle, the sovereign, just God is challenged for unjust, human suffering. We humans are subject to pain and distress in ways that are contrary to God's own will, so why doesn't God do something to secure our well-being?

Of course, theologians and preachers offer a range of interpretations of God's good news in relation to human suffering, a range of explanations to the question of theodicy, especially given the fact that this question has been a driving force in the evolution of Western theology throughout the history of the church. Those who claim that God literally created the world *ex nihilo* must deal with it differently than those who hold that such language is symbolic, metaphorical, or mythological. At one end of the spectrum, some attempt to address the question in terms of limited human perception and understanding of the mystery of God and the ways of the universe, such as claiming that finite human beings are unable to see the big picture of creation as God does and thus suffering only seems to be unjust or unnecessary. At the other end, some modify the traditional understanding of the nature of God, such as claiming that God is all-loving but not all-powerful.

It is beyond the scope of this work to explore all the various options in relation to the question of theodicy or to make a constructive argument for one approach against all the others. It is important to recognize, however, that across the theological spectrum all would agree that our suffering is not the last word on this dimension of the human condition. In some way or another (depending on the preacher's hermeneutical approach to scripture and history), the story of Christ's resurrection reminds us that God gets the last word. By raising Christ from the dead, God addresses the absolute limit of human finitude and suffering: mortality. An empty tomb trumps theodicy every time.

By this last claim, I do not mean to suggest, however, that we turn suffering into a trifling matter. The claim that the resurrection is part of God's answer to suffering does not solve the problem of theodicy. We continue to suffer and even die in spite of the fact that our faith states emphatically, "Christ is risen indeed!" The claim simply asserts that suffering, whatever one's theological orientation, can only be understood from a Christian point of view *in light of* God's salvific concern and care for us, which is demonstrated ultimately in the story of Christ's resurrection.

To deny or ignore the reality, depth, and breadth of human suffering is to be theologically and existentially dishonest. Individuals face physical illness, including pain and injury, as well as emotional struggle, including mental illness and spiritual distress. At the corporate level, we are inflicted with economic and social inequality, war, and natural disaster. We experience diverse examples of such suffering, witness forms of suffering beyond our experience, are always aware of the possibility of more and new forms of suffering just around the corner. Sometimes our suffering is mild and manageable, and other times it is intense and unbearable. To ignore or deny such suffering in our theology and sermons is to make claims of God's salvific love into cheap sentimentalism.

We trust in the resurrecting God enough to question God when our experience in the death-dealing world seems to contradict our understanding of God as just and merciful. Scripture models such faithful questioning well. As Walter Brueggemann says, "Theodicy is a constant concern of the entire Bible."[6]

Biblical

The Hebrew Bible is certainly filled with such concern. In chapter 1 we mentioned the huge number of lament psalms in which those praying at times hold God responsible for suffering and always recognize that God alone can alleviate suffering.[7] Texts of God's judgment raise questions of God's responsibility for suffering, such as when Abraham challenges God's decision to destroy Sodom (Gen 18:16-33) or prophetic explanations of Israel's or Judah's political situation being a result of God removing divine favor from the chosen people. The most extensive investigations of the problem of God's justice in relation to human suffering in the canon are found in Habakkuk, Ecclesiastes, and especially Job. These texts are not preached often enough.

The New Testament, likewise, raises the question of theodicy regularly. In Matthew, Jesus claims that God makes the sun shine and the rain fall on the just and the unjust alike (Matt 5:45). In Luke, Jesus associates violence at the hands of Pilate with the tragic fall of a tower in Siloam in a way that raises the question (Luke 13:1-5). Apocalyptic literature as a genre raises the question of theodicy, but nowhere is it more explicit than in Revelation when the martyrs in heaven cry out asking how long God will allow persecution to continue (Rev 6:9-11). And nowhere in the Bible as a whole is the pathos of anguish in the midst of suffering experienced by the Christian reader more powerfully than when Jesus cries out in the words of Psalm 22, "My God, my God, why have you left me?" from the cross just before he dies (Matt 27:46; Mark 15:34).

---

6. Walter Brueggemann, "Theodicy in a Social Dimension," *Journal for the Study of the Old Testament* 10 (33): 3–25.

7. P. 8; on preaching lament, see Sally A. Brown and Patrick D. Miller, eds., *Lament: Reclaiming Practices in Pulpit, Pew, and Public Square* (Louisville: Westminster John Knox, 2005).

Of course, many biblical texts in both testaments that do not explicitly name the question of theodicy deal with suffering in relation to the vertical dimension. Some of these still wear the question of theodicy on their sleeves—for instance, who can read of the flood destroying almost the entirety of the human race or of God hardening Pharaoh's heart so that he continued persecuting the Israelites and not ask questions about God's justice and love? Others do not draw close to the theological question so much as to simply name angst over disorder, pain, destruction, and death in a way that we turn to God for comfort and hope. Human suffering in some form or another that impacts our relationship with God can be found on almost every page of the canon. While we need to deal with suffering in relation to theodicy explicitly from the pulpit in a cumulative fashion, we also need to deal with these other expressions related to suffering in a cumulative fashion. They still indirectly address the question of theodicy, but the sermon may be focused directly on a different level of experience and concern.

These kinds of texts, from across the canon, look at evil and suffering directly, with anguished honesty that refuses to flinch. But they also affirm God's sovereignty and goodness even while asking, "Why God?" and "How long, O God?" Prayers of lament include praise of the Divine One who saves. God answers Job from the whirlwind. Judgment oracles are followed by promises of eschatological salvation. In the Sermon on the Mount after Jesus reminds the hearers that the rain falls on the good and bad alike, Jesus instructs them not to worry but to consider the lilies (Matt 6:25-34). And after Jesus dies on the cross with a cry of abandonment, God raises him from the dead on the third day. Biblically, the question of theodicy is never the last word. But neither do the responses provided erase the question, tying up the theology in a nice, pretty bow. They do not put a fresh coat of paint on the world to cover the scars of suffering. The Bible challenges and proclaims God's lovingkindness in the same breath, making clear that both—held in the strongest of theological tensions—are necessary, faithful responses the human condition. We need to carry this very tension into our preaching if our hearers are to experience the depth of their lives named and addressed without either horrifying cynicism or sugary sentimentalism. The goal is to name the harsh realities of human suffering in light of the reality of divine hope.

Homiletical

Whereas it is difficult to convince a congregation that they are idolaters, there is no real difficulty in getting a congregation to reflect on their suffering. Getting them to raise the question of theodicy may be another matter, however. As we have noted, many raise the question when life forces it upon them. For others, however, they have been taught and internalized the idea that such questioning is a form of unfaithfulness. Indeed, these may well consider asking the question aloud to be a sinful challenge to the sovereignty of God. Thus preachers must give parishioners permission and empower them to raise the question of God's justice in light of human suffering, in light of their own pain. There are two essential components to doing this effectively in the pulpit, both of which require a cumulative approach, that is, both require repetition in the pulpit stretched out for many a Sunday.

First, preachers simply need to show those who fear doubting God that there is biblical precedent for asking the question of theodicy. As an authority for faith, the Bible provides a clear model for us even asking about the fairness of God in relation to the human condition. If patriarchs, psalmists, and prophets do it, who are we to think it is a mode of unfaithfulness?

Second, preachers must model such questioning themselves. If we treat the question of theodicy in the pulpit as an abstract theological issue that we examine at arm's length, the hearers will not trust us with their deepest questioning. We must model such questioning for them by inviting them into our existential concerns about God's justice in light of suffering. To keep the sermon from becoming about us and being experienced as some therapeutic moment in which the hearers offer pastoral care for the preacher, however, we must avoid talking too much about our own suffering. If we do, we need to make sure it is suffering with which our hearers can identify so that their focus remains on their own suffering and not on the preacher's. A cleaner approach is for preachers to name our very real questioning in relation to suffering we witness as a pastor, Christian, and human being. This puts a little distance between the preacher and the suffering but not between the preacher and the questioning.

To extend further the idea of sharing suffering the preacher witnesses, we can note that we address this question of theodicy over and over again in relation to varying types of suffering—illness, discrimination, relational pain, disabilities, natural disasters, mental illness, economic disparity, spiritual anxiety, isolation, persecution, and death. While we will deal with moral evil in the chapter on the horizontal dimension of the human condition, it also belongs here alongside natural evil. As surely as God created (speaking literally or figuratively) the weather systems that result in tsunamis that wipe out populations, God created humans who injure other humans. Only by dealing with a wide range of examples of suffering cumulatively will we help our parishioners think through the issue and reality of suffering in a systematic way that will help them respond to both their own and to others' suffering in a faithful manner. On this Sunday someone may not identify experientially with the specific kinds of suffering we name and think about the issue on a more abstract level. On that Sunday, the person may have a visceral identification with the kinds of suffering we mention and relate to the topic on a more emotional level. Both are needed for people to be made whole in dealing with the question of theodicy.

As we have noted above, however, the preacher does not preach on suffering alone but on God's good news in relation to human suffering. Death is never the last word for the Christian preacher. Out of our particular theological orientations, we preachers must offer congregations a theological worldview that deals with human suffering in a pastorally empathetic and theologically consistent manner.

Yet our theological responses to theodicy must leave room for our hearers to construct other responses. In other words, the preacher's response should be directive and suggestive but never be presented as the final word on the matter. If our theology doesn't accord with the hearers' experience and is expressed in a take-it-or-leave-it form, the hearers will leave it. Instead, we offer a theological proposal for our hearers to consider in the midst of their own seeking of an answer. Perhaps they will embrace our theology. Maybe they will adapt it. Or maybe they will reject it but in doing so they take a stronger step toward a theological understanding that better informs their life of faith.

They cannot do any of these if we do not offer a theological proposal. We must be wary of models of ministry that so emphasize pastors accompanying those suffering that they feel relieved of the responsibility to speak to that suffering. I remember a professor of pastoral care preaching in a seminary chapel service on the issue of suffering. As he began his sermon and the topic became clear, I thought to myself, *Here comes a touchy-feely approach to ministry to those in pain.* But the preacher told a story of a friend dying when he was in graduate school. He struggled with the loss. He struggled with God's role in the death. He sat grieving with a professor who was serving as a pastor to him. The professor promised to be with him through this, to which the student replied, "With all due respect, I don't need you. What I need is a word from God." A ministry of presence is nothing but a vaporous fog surrounding the suffering if it is not accompanied by a ministry of word. Pastors need not claim to have the final or only word dealing with theodicy to be able to offer a meaningful word.

This meaningful word needs to be offered from the pulpit as much in times when a crisis of faith caused by suffering is not at hand as it does in times of immediate pain. Preaching on the question of suffering right after a tragedy meets an immediate kind of pastoral need, like a funeral naming the pain of loss and the hope of resurrection following a death. But preaching on theodicy when a crisis has not evoked the questions allows hearers to consider the matter apart from the deluge of emotional, physical, psychological, and spiritual hardship in which we drown during a crisis. In other words, preaching about suffering when our hearers are not suffering intensely will equip them for when those times of crisis arise. It will give them the ability to recall a word, to speak a word, a meaningful word, out of their own faithful but hurting being.

Sample Sermon

The following sermon was not delivered in relation to any particular instance of suffering or crisis. Instead it is an example of one that deals with the question of theodicy in a general fashion to help inform the theological thinking of the congregation. It raises the question of God's fairness in relation to historical and contemporary events not so much to propose an answer as to give the congregation permission to ask the question as a faith stance. The sermon does so by teaching the congregation how a psalm of lament (Ps 94) functions and serves as a biblical model for worship and faith today.

It was about 430 . . . not the time . . . the year. It was about the year 430 in the Roman Empire . . . to be specific in a monastery in northern Egypt. There was a young novice there named Brother . . . umm . . . Fred. I know the name is a little odd but he's a fictional monk, so why not a fictional name? In Latin he was Brother Fredicus.

Anyway, Brother Fred had been in the monastery for just under a year. It was nearing the time for him to move from being a novice to being ordained as a full-blown monk. He would make vows that would bind him to this community, its beliefs, and its practices for the rest of his living days.

But part of one of those practices was making him question whether he wanted to make that commitment or not. You see, in the monastery, they prayed together eight times a day for a total of fifty-six prayer services a week and almost three thousand times a year. Today, we call that practice the liturgy of the hours. Anyway, they prayed this much to fulfill Paul's command to pray unceasingly. But the amount of prayer required wasn't the part that was giving Fred a hard time.

An element of this practice of unceasing prayer was to pray the entire Psalter every week—all 150 psalms were read or chanted—about 21 psalms a day. But praying the psalms every week wasn't the part that was giving Fred a hard time.

At some services, they prayed the same psalm every day at exactly the same time of the day. For example, at the prayer service right before dawn, they chanted Psalm 94 every day. It was sort of part of an extended call to worship. Every day. Every single day. First service of the day. This was the part that gave Fred a hard time. Psalm 94 every day troubled Brother Fred deeply.

Oh, he knew why they prayed it every day. It was because of verses 16 and 17. I think you have the psalm written out as a bulletin insert if you want to look at it. Verses 16-17 read, *"Who will stand up for me against the wicked? Who will help me against evildoers? If the Lord hadn't helped me, I would live instantly in total silence."*

"Total silence" is a metaphor for death. So the monks prayed Psalm 94 as a prayer of thanksgiving that God protected them through the night so they might live to see another day. These two lines could be read as sort of the reversed, waking-up version of

> Now I lay me down to sleep,
> I pray the Lord my soul to keep.

I guess the morning version would beomething like,

> In my sleep I did not die;
> I thank the Lord for drawing nigh.

So Brother Fred understood why Psalm 94 was prayed every dawn. In fact, he liked those two verses. It was the rest of the psalm that troubled him.

The prayer starts off complaining to God. It's a lament.

> Lord, avenging God—
> > avenging God, show yourself!
> Rise up, judge of the earth!
> > Pay back the arrogant exactly what they
> > > deserve!
> How long will the wicked—oh, Lord!—
> > how long will the wicked win?
> They spew arrogant words;
> > all the evildoers are bragging.
> They crush your own people, Lord!
> > They abuse your very own possession.
> They kill widows and immigrants;
> > they murder orphans,
> > saying all the while,
> > "The Lord can't see it;
> > Jacob's God doesn't know
> > what's going on!" (vv. 1-7)

To start off your day every day calling God to bring vindication on the arrogant and wicked ones of the world is no easy thing.

Now mind you, Brother Fredicus knew that these wicked ones were out there wreaking havoc on the world. He hadn't always lived in a monastery after all. In fact, before coming to the monastery he worked for the *Cairo Town News-Graphic* as a reporter.

- He wrote stories on corrupt politicians doing what was best for contributors to their campaigns instead of what was best for the people.
- He wrote about pastors who embezzled from their congregations.
- He wrote about men who abused their wives, about citizens running immigrants off for stealing their jobs, about sex slave traders,

about one country invading another without just
   cause,
about payday loan companies preying on the poor.
• He wrote about theft
and slander
and drunk driving
and murder
and treason
and every kind of oppression you can imagine.

Fred wrote about it until he said "No more!" and decided to withdraw from the world and become a monk.

But even out in that chapel in the desert, every day, he
had to pray about the wicked in the world. And praying Psalm 94, every day, he had to accuse God of not
doing anything about them. He felt unfaithful accusing
God about taking too long to do something about the
evil in the world, to take down those who were arrogant
enough to think they could stand up to God.

So he had a problem with the next section of the psalm as
well, because it turns from talking to God about evildoers
to addressing the evildoers directly. The psalmist ends the
previous section by saying that evildoers don't think God
perceives what they're doing since there doesn't seem
to be any retribution. And now the psalmist says, "You
don't think God perceives? Well, perceive this, buster!"

You ignorant people better learn quickly.
      You fools—when will you get some sense?
The one who made the ear,
      can't he hear?
The one who formed the eye,
      can't he see?
The one who disciplines nations,
      can't he punish?
The one who teaches humans,
      doesn't he know?
The Lord does indeed know human thoughts,
      knows that they are nothing but a puff of air.
   (vv. 8-11)

Fred didn't mind calling down the wicked. He actually liked that idea a lot. He especially liked the idea of quoting the Bible to do it. The problem was that he wasn't sure the warning had any teeth. The wicked seem to have a point: God doesn't seem to be a God of vindication. In fact, isn't that what the psalmist just had us complaining about in the first stanza of the psalm?

- The widows,
  the orphans,
  the immigrants—they don't seem to be vindicated.
- The victims of racism,
  ageism,
  heterosexism,
  classism
  and sexism—they don't seem to be vindicated.
- Those who have lost their pensions,
  or who are scared to go to the market
    because a car bomb might go off,
  or who are bullied in school or harassed at work
  —God doesn't seem to vindicate them.

Brother Fredicus was so troubled by all of this that just before he was to make his vows to become a monk, he went to the abbot and asked why anyone would want to pray this lament first thing in the morning from now until eternity. Brother Fred told the abbot how uncomfortable he felt complaining to God in the first stanza. And he told him how uncomfortable he felt speaking to the evildoers in the second stanza. And he said, "You really want me to pray that?"

The old abbot smiled and responded to Fred, "You do know I didn't write the Bible, don't you? This prayer is not mine to invite you into. Psalm 94 has been prayed by Jews for nearly a millennium. It's been prayed by Christians for four hundred years. This prayer is yours whether you pray it here in the monastery with us or not. You can't escape this prayer out in the world any more than you can escape the world here in worship."

Fred started to respond, but the abbot just kept on talking. He said, "You can't focus on just the first two stanzas. After the psalmist addresses the evildoers, he turns back to talk to God but this time he talks about the faithful who follow the Torah:

> The people you discipline, Lord, are truly happy—
>> the ones you teach from your Instruction—
>> giving them relief from troubling times
>>> until a pit is dug for the wicked.
> The Lord will not reject his people;
>> he will not abandon his very own possession.
> No, but justice will once again meet up with
> righteousness,
>> and all whose heart is right will follow after.
> (vv. 12-15)

"See," the abbot said, "the psalmist celebrates that even though the wicked seem to be winning the day, God's justice will get the last word. God won't turn away from the covenant with God's people. Justice will return to those who strive to live faithful, righteous lives. Wickedness will not win. God always gets the last word. God always is the last word."

Fred tried to jump in again, but the abbot was on a roll now. You couldn't have stopped that fifth-century fictional monk any more than you could stop a revival preacher calling sinners down to the altar rail as the choir sings the twenty-seventh verse of "Just as I Am." He kept going: "The fourth stanza of the psalm brings God's last word home to roost. In it the psalmist turns from talking about the world generally, the wicked generally, the righteous generally, and gets personal. He prays about himself.

> Who will stand up for me against the wicked?
>> Who will help me against evildoers?
> If the Lord hadn't helped me,
>> I would live instantly in total silence.
> Whenever I feel my foot slipping,
>> your faithful love steadies me, Lord.

When my anxieties multiply,
>your comforting calms me down.

Can a wicked ruler be your ally;
>one who wreaks havoc by means of the law?

The wicked gang up against the lives of the righteous.
>They condemn innocent blood.

But the LORD is my fortress;
>my God is my rock of refuge.

He will repay them for their wickedness,
>completely destroy them because of their evil.

Yes, the LORD our God will completely destroy them.
>(vv. 16-23)

"The general accusations that opened the prayer have now given way to the statement of personal trust that ends the prayer.

- You stand up against the wicked for me.
- You keep me from living in total silence.
- Your love keeps me secure when I am insecure.
- Your comfort gives me relief when I am burdened down with worry.
- You are my fortress.
- You are my rock.

"You see, when we pray, every day, we can and should complain to God as long as the world God created has evil in it that causes suffering. But every day when we complain, we should also offer to God our devotion and trust."

Brother Fred seemed to be pondering this as if he were close to getting it. He had a lightbulb over his head but it wasn't yet lit—and not just because lightbulbs hadn't been invented yet in 430. So to help him the rest of the way, the abbot told him a story. He said, "In the year 1944, Elie Wiesel was a fifteen-year-old Jew whom the Nazis had imprisoned at Auschwitz. His mother and sisters had been gassed. He was forced to do hard labor every day without much food, knowing that if he didn't measure up, he'd be killed. He watched beatings and hangings every single day he was there. In addition to

---

63

fearing for his life, he didn't know what to make of all this. He didn't know where God was in all of it.

"There were three rabbis who were in Elie's bunk house at Auschwitz. The religious leaders experienced and saw the same things Elie experienced and saw every day. They feared death the same way Elie did, every day. And finally one night, they put God on trial. All through the night, they argued about whether or not God was responsible for the Holocaust. They cited scripture and named the horrors they had experienced in the same breath. And as the night came to a close, they had closing arguments, and then they pronounced God guilty. And then do you know what they did? As dawn was drawing near, they prayed, just like they did every day. It was probably the Modeh Ani, the traditional prayer Jews say just as they awake. It's a short, two-line prayer that speaks of sleeping as a sort of death and gives thanks to God for the gift of life for another day. It goes like this:

> I offer thanks before you, living and eternal king,
> for you have mercifully restored my soul within me;
> Your faithfulness is great.

"Kind of sounds like this:

> In my sleep I did not die;
> I thank the Lord for drawing nigh.

"Kind of sounds like this:

> If the LORD had not been my help,
> my soul would soon have lived in total silence."

The day after Brother Fred had the conversation with his abbot, he took his vows and became a monk—dedicating his life to praying unceasingly on behalf of the world. And he's been praying Psalm 94 every morning since the year 430.

- He prayed it when the Huns were invading the Roman Empire.

- He prayed it during the Crusades and during the Inquisition.
- He prayed it as Europe colonized, enslaved, and killed peoples from around the globe.
- He prayed it during the Civil War, World War I, World War II, the Korean War, and the Vietnam War.
- He prayed it on 9/11 and when fighting began in Afghanistan and Iraq.
- He prayed it during the Arab Spring.
- He prayed Psalm 94 every day this week,

  - when a drunk driver plowed into a music festival crowd in Austin, Texas;
  - when commentators wondered if terrorists had control of a Malaysian Airline plane;
  - when the Russian army marched into Crimea;
  - when a study was released that showed massive racial disparity in American public schools still exists;
  - when a college student was arrested for making ricin in his dorm room;
  - when protestors were killed in the streets of Venezuela.

Every single day for almost sixteen hundred years, Brother Fredicus has risen before dawn and started his day by complaining to God about the state of the world and then by expressing his personal and ultimate trust in that very same God. And he told me when I talked to him on the phone this morning that he'd be glad to have us join him any time we're ready to embrace that kind of faith.

THE HORIZONTAL DIMENSION
OF THE HUMAN CONDITION

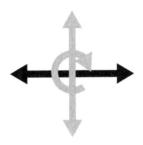

Our overarching concern in this book is with the preacher's task of proclaiming how God's good news addresses the human condition, that is, the threats and damage done to the physical, intellectual, psychological, spiritual, material, and social well-being of human beings individually and human communities collectively. We are using the greatest commandment—"You must love the Lord your God with all your heart, with all your being, with all your mind, and with all your strength. . . . You will love your neighbor as yourself'" (Mark 12:30-31)—as a heuristic lens through which to view and bring the three dimensions of the human condition into a cumulative homiletical approach.

In this chapter, we are focusing specifically on the horizontal dimension of the human condition implied in the command to love our neighbor as ourselves. This command is intensified by the Golden Rule (Matt 7:12//Luke 6:31) and radicalized by the instruction to love our enemies (Matt 5:43-48//Luke 6:27-36). The very fact that humanity must be commanded to love others in the same way that we care for ourselves implies that we do not do so. There is brokenness in the relationships in the human species, individually and corporately, that threatens and damages our well-being. We experience this brokenness from both sides. We fail to love others and others fail in loving us. We sin against others and suffer when others sin against us. This horizontal dimension of our model of the human condition focuses on ethics in relationships between individuals and human communities, and we will examine both sin and suffering in relation to it.

Brokenness in the relationships between human individuals, communities, and societies is the usual starting point for dealing with the human condition by some theologians and preachers in various strands of liberal theology who claim a corporate approach to anthropology as the best starting point for doing theology—for example, social gospel and liberation schools of thought as well as some approaches to process and revisionist theologies. There is a good rationale behind this emphasis in that it recognizes the central role personal and social ethics play in scripture, tradition, and Christian practice. For preachers who hold the horizontal dimension as primary for understanding the human condition, the vertical and inner dimensions are seen as derivative of the vertical. In other words, if the core problem of the human condition is seen as brokenness in the relationships with our neighbors, then this brokenness in turn causes brokenness in relationships between humanity and God and in the relationship of a person with her- or himself. Conversely, for those who hold that either of the other two dimensions are primary for understanding the human condition theologically, the horizontal dimension is seen as resulting from either brokenness in the relationship with God or an inner brokenness.

Regardless of where one starts, however, any description of the human condition or cumulative preaching that fails to deal adequately with sin and suffering in the ethical dimension offers only a partial and thus flawed understanding of the situation in which we humans exist. After all, sinning against our neighbor is a sin against God and causes damage to our (and others') inner self. Likewise, suffering on the horizontal plane raises questions about why God allows us to suffer at the hands of others and is inseparable from inner suffering.

Of course, thinkers in the different schools that start with this dimension cannot be reduced to similarities in all the ways they approach the horizontal dimension of the human condition. There are significant differences in the theological worldviews and ethical methodologies of these schools of thought. For example, the starting point for making ethical judgments and claims can be quite varied—ranging from Jesus's proclamation of God's reign to the experience of a particular marginalized community. Some may argue for a utilitarian approach to making ethical decisions and acting ethically, while others operate with a deontological approach.

Still, in one way or another, scholars and preachers dealing with this dimension of the human condition emphasize, theologically speaking, the justice of God. God is the righteous judge who condemns those who abuse power, liberates the oppressed, and cares for the downtrodden. God wills the good for all and commands humanity to care for the good for all. While different thinkers and schools name the ways God works in the world to achieve these goals differently, they agree that God is in some way striving to move the world toward an eschatological vision of fairness, peace, equality, mercy, and love. As Alpha and Omega, God not only brought the world into being but has a good purpose (*telos*) for the world and for us humans who inhabit it that involves us being in right relationship with one another.

Expressed conversely from the human side, theology focusing on the horizontal dimension recognizes that our well-being is inextricably related to human interdependence. Humanity, made in the image of the Triune God, is a social species. We do not act, think, or feel in a vacuum but always in relation to the ways we have been treated and constructed by other individuals, families, communities, cultures, and so on; and others act, think, and feel in relation to the way we and others have treated and constructed them. In other words, everything that humans do is in response to God's gift of the interconnectedness of humanity, whether we recognize it or not. God calls us to act toward the other, individually and corporately, with an ethic of *agape* (Greek for "unconditional love")[1] or *hesed* (Hebrew for "steadfast lovingkindness").[2] Humans, however, corrupt God's gift of interdependence resulting in both sin and suffering.

Sin

Theological

We fail miserably in loving our neighbors and enemies. Sin in this vertical dimension is shaped by acts of injuring others—our threatening and damaging the well-being of our fellow humans. We are self-centered, selfish, and self-serving beings, looking out for ourselves and for those closest to us. In one way or another, we exert power over the other instead of using whatever power and resources we have on behalf of the other.

We commit a wide range of sinful actions against our neighbors; but structurally speaking, to use the construct made famous by Martin Buber, every unethical act toward another (individually) or toward others (corporately) is one in which we treat others as objects to be consumed and/or discarded for personal gain (Its) instead of as subjects of worth (Thous) to be engaged with respect and love for mutual benefit.[3] The second half of the Decalogue deals with this dimension—we dishonor our parents, murder, commit adultery, steal, bear false witness, and covet when it profits us without regard for the God-given worth and rights of the other. To break any of these commandments is to place ourselves and our desires before the well-being of our neighbors. The fact is that no matter

---

1. For example, see Gene Outka, *Agape: An Ethical Analysis*, Yale Publications in Religion 17 (New Haven: Yale University Press, 1972).

2. For example, see Emily Askew and O. Wesley Allen, Jr., *Beyond Heterosexism in the Pulpit* (Eugene, OR: Cascade, 2015), 20–32.

3. Martin Buber, *I and Thou*, trans. Ronald G. Smith (New York: Scribner, 1958).

how well intentioned we are when we say that we will commit "to do justice, embrace faithful love, and walk humbly with [our] God" (Mic 6:8), we fail over and over again and are unable to succeed in our willingness and ability to live out an ethic of love.

So thoroughly sinful are we in this dimension that our sin is manifest at different levels, from hurting an individual close to us to participation in systemic structures that oppress masses of unknown people. It extends from hurling out an insult in an argument with one's partner to genocide of an entire people, and a whole host of injuries in between. Moreover, it includes both intentional and unintentional or even undesired harm done to others. It includes a purposeful act of violence against another individual as well as being forced by one's income to buy cheaper school clothes for one's children when the cost of those clothes is dependent upon child labor in another part of the world, where children make less than a living wage and work in unsafe and deplorable circumstances.

Grouping all of these different examples together is not to claim that they are equal in their harm—clearly a verbal jab does not threaten someone's well-being to the same degree that bombing a civilian population does. Grouping them together is simply to name that *structurally speaking* the preacher can view these sorts of examples as all existing on the same theological, horizontal plane in our three-dimensional model.

Our failure in our horizontal relationships with our neighbors, however, is not the last word on this dimension of the human condition. Our sinful nature is answered by God's character. The God of justice speaks louder than our injustice. God's mercy is stronger than our lack of compassion. God's peace outlives our tendencies toward violence. And God's love is wider than our hatred. As the quote goes, made famous in recent times by Martin Luther King Jr., "The arc of the moral universe is long, but it bends towards justice."[4]

---

4. While the line is older than King, it is often quoted from his use of it in his sermon to Temple Israel in Hollywood, California, on February 26, 1965. The speech can be found at www.americanrhetoric.com/speeches/mlktempleisraelhollywood.htm. Accessed November 11, 2015.

Biblical

The Hebrew Bible, especially the Torah and the Prophets, is filled with commandments, teachings, and oracles instructing Israelites individually and corporately to act and live ethically toward others. These instructions are concerned with both care for the neighbor and for the moral, ethical identity of the people of Israel. Israel was to be a people made up of not only individuals who observed feasts and the Sabbath but also caregivers for the widow and orphan, land owners who left a portion of the harvest in the fields for gleaning, and kings who ruled with fairness.

While these are certainly instructions to be followed, biblical writers do not view them as burdens placed on the Israelites by God. Nay, they are gifts from God. Others' lives may be defined by hatred and selfishness, but "our" lives get to be defined by love, justice, and charity! Nowhere is this more celebrated than in Psalm 119, where the psalmist longs to know and follow God's law better because he delights in it more than in gold. Notice all the terms the author uses praising the law: it is a blessing, is an answer to prayer, melts away sorrow, revives, gives peace and hope, keeps one steady, is a source of deep understanding, is a guide, is an inheritance from God, and gives life. Ethical instruction gives life! In other words, the law is salvation—God spares our life *so that* we may keep God's decrees (v. 88).

Likewise, the New Testament vision of the Christ event can be interpreted through the lens of the horizontal dimension of the human condition as an expression of God's work of reconciling us to one another. God's justice and peace are revealed in Jesus's ministry and death, where Christ is presented as the exemplar of the ethical life. Christ's proclamation of the advent of God's reign is a vision for a just and peaceful society, over against Caesar's reign. Christ's ethical teaching is countercultural in the manner in which it calls for radical care of the other—fulfilling, not abandoning, the law of the Hebrew Bible. And Christ's refusal to engage in violence against Caesar in order to bring about God's reign is an example of the way

Christians are to best engage evil in the world. So the Christ event calls us to the good and makes possible that good by revealing to us the way.

This last idea—that the Christ event makes an ethical existence possible—is especially important. Too often ethical and social justice kinds of sermons offer a call to ethical ways of being that are more motivational speeches based on humanistic terms than proclamation of God's good news, as if humans can and should simply choose to be better persons and make better societies. On the backside of the Enlightenment and in the shadow of the Holocaust, however, we cannot be so naïve to think Paul got it wrong when he says, for all of us, "I don't do the good that I want to do, but I do the evil that I don't want to do" (Rom 7:19). Paul makes clear that whatever good we do on the horizontal plane, God has empowered us through Christ to do it. After bemoaning that we do not do what we want to do (that is, adhere to the law, which includes the call for the ethical life) because sin dwells in us (v. 17), Paul asks, "Who will rescue me from this body of death?" and responds with a doxology: "Thanks be to God through Jesus Christ our Lord!" (vv. 24-25 NRSV). He goes on to declare that by taking on the likeness of our sinful flesh, Christ dealt with sin, allowing the spirit of God to dwell in us in the place of sin (8:1-17). We do not lead an ethical life by our own abilities, or to save ourselves. The ethical life is a gift from God.

This view of ethics as a gift can be read in the background, then, of all of Paul's paraenetical material. In almost all of his letters, Paul includes ethical advice (paraenesis) toward the end. He deals with pastoral and theological issues first and then turns to exhortation. This statement is, of course, an oversimplification of the form of Paul's letters—hortatory material is mixed in with pastoral and theological material earlier in the letters and good news is offered in the midst of ethical instruction later in the letters. Still, the point is clear enough: good news invites good works for Paul, not the reverse; but neither does Paul's proclamation (say, of justification by faith) preclude a concern for ethical behavior. Paul is neither a libertarian nor a moral philosopher. He is a Christian preacher concerned with both salvation wrought by grace and the ethical life that is a gift of that salvation. For Paul, then, like the Hebrew Bible, the ethical life has as much to do with the identity of the community of faith as it does with concern for the treatment of the neighbor. The church, as the body of Christ, is (must be by definition) an ethical community.

Homiletical

Our preaching must also, then, include an ethical element if we are to help build up the church into who we are as defined by God's good news.

The problem for much of contemporary preaching, however, is that we do too much of this. Far too many sermons today are moral or ethical in their orientation. We substitute exhortation for proclamation. We do this because we are heirs to the Puritan approach to preaching. The Puritan Plain Form of the sermon is one with which we are all familiar whether we recognize that label or not. In this form, the sermon begins with *exegesis* of a biblical text, moves to a general (universal) theological *interpretation* based on that exegesis, and then concludes with an *application* of that broad interpretation to the specific congregation being addressed.[5] This "application" need not be moral or ethical exhortation, but it usually is. In fact, it is so much the case that laity have learned the approach by rote. Lead a Bible study on almost any text, offer them exegetical observations about the text, ask them what the text means for us today, and they will usually answer in terms of something we ought to *do*. Application has come to mean applying to our behavior as opposed to applying a certain perspective on God's character or on the work and person of Christ to our particular circumstances. In more conservative theological traditions this application is usually concerned

5. See O. Wesley Allen, Jr., *Determining the Form*, Elements of Preaching (Minneapolis: Fortress, 2008), 29–37; and Ronald J. Allen, ed., *Patterns of Preaching: A Sermon Sampler* (St. Louis: Chalice, 1998), 7–13.

with individual moral and ethical behavior, while in more progressive pulpits it is concerned with social ethical behavior. While the particular moral and ethical issues on which conservatives and progressives preach are often different, the homiletical strategy is nearly identical: move from exegesis of the ancient text to contemporary behavioral application.

There are two reasons this homiletical strategy is problematic. One is theological/exegetical in nature and the other homiletical.

The first is that many of the biblical texts on which we preachers are basing such exhortation are not themselves concerned with ethical behavior. There are plenty of texts that are concerned with ethical behavior of both the individual and the social types. When we preach on those texts we should absolutely raise ethical concerns. But when a text tells a story, makes a theological claim about the nature of salvation, or offers a prayer of praise to the transcendent God, the preacher should not tie it to a chair and beat it with a hose in order to coerce a confession against its will that it is really concerned with ethics after all.[6]

The second problem with an overabundance of ethical preaching is that it dulls the ears of our congregations. As surely as parishioners start reaching for the hymnal when a preacher says, "And my third point is . . ." they stop listening when every sermon turns to shoulds, oughts, and musts near the end. A cumulative approach to preaching requires variation along with repetition. Repetition alone becomes more like white noise than an exclamation point. When was the last time you listened to the content of the daily repeated testing of the Emergency Broadcast System? Every good preacher knows that if people in the pews seem to not be listening, you do not get louder saying the same thing over and over. You pause. In silence. A break in the middle of the sermon invites people back in when for one reason or another they have left it. Likewise, breaks

---

6. Thanks to Anna Carter Florence for first "applying" this image from Billy Collins's poem "Introduction to Poetry" to preaching as found in "Put Away Your Sword! Taking the Torture out of the Sermon," in *What's the Matter with Preaching Today?*, ed. Mike Graves (Louisville: Westminster John Knox, 2004), 93–108.

between ethical sermons will invite people who view such sermons as preachy, boring, the same old same old, to enter into them again with fresh ears.

When they do so, we need to make sure their return is worth the effort. It is important to deal with weighty moral and ethical issues, but it is a waste of the listeners' time to be moralistic in the pulpit. There is a reason "preachy" is a bad word. It implies a looking down at others from on high with an attitude of self-righteousness that tells others how to better themselves (i.e., how to better act like me). The key to preaching ethics without being preachy in relation to ethics is, as with all preaching, to show, not tell. There are three elements of this showing to highlight in this context.

First, as implied in what was just said, preachers must not hold up a mirror to the congregation while standing behind it. We must preach from the same side of the mirror, from a posture in which our sinful reflection is shown right alongside the reflections of everyone else. This does not mean, however, that we need not put all our peccadillos and unholy actions on display. As preachers should not use the pulpit to stand on a pedestal above the congregation, neither should we turn it into a confessional in which we seek absolution from those in the pews. Instead, we need to include ourselves in portrayals of sin in the vertical dimension in ways that we identify with the congregation and they with us.

Second, we must show the *need* for ethical behavior. Too often preachers call for this or that action as if the need is self-evident. Or if we do speak of a need, it is in terms of what the recipient will receive from our action. The insulted will gain respect. The poor will be fed. The oppressed will gain rights. Such results are, of course, good in their own right, but homiletically they do not address the dimension of the human condition on which we are focusing. At the moment we are concerned with our sin in relation to their suffering, and that sin is what is so often not shown in ethical sermons.

When we sin in the horizontal dimension, we cause the suffering of others. We need not only show someone who has been insulted so that we feel empathy for the person but show him or her in a way that we take account of the insulting we have done. We need not only show how hungry some are so that our congregation's heart (rightfully so) breaks for them but also show how our abundance is directly related to their lack. We need not only show how a group is oppressed by racism, classicism, heterosexism, ableism, or sexism so that we feel a sense of righteous indignation (which we should). We should also show how our privilege rests on the necks of those who do not have the same confluence of privilege we in this congregation possess. It is too easy in the face of individual and structural suffering of others to feel Christian charity toward them while at the same time denying any role in their suffering.

To put it bluntly, we need to offer sermons in which those in our pews are invited not only to feel bad *for* others who suffer but to feel bad *about* our participation in making them suffer. We need to feel a sense of guilt because we are actually guilty. But this may take some convincing since much of our guilt may be due to indirect sin more than direct. An old quote goes something like, "The extra coat in my closet is taken off the back of someone who does not have one."[7] I did not take a coat from anyone, but my excess is related to others' lack in ways I cannot see or experience directly. Thus, I, Wes Allen, did not tell any police officer to shoot a young man because he was black. I did not discriminate against a transgender person. I did not hinder a Third World country from developing more quickly in industrial and technological production. But I do enjoy the benefits—as a white, cisgender, middle-aged, middle-class, North American male—of not being suspect of wrongdoing simply because of my skin color, of not fearing emotional or physical abuse based on what public bathroom I choose to use, and of wearing my clothes that are produced in countries where people labor for long, long hours without making a living wage. My sin is indirect but it is real sin. I do not simply feel guilty; I am guilty.

---

7. Source unknown.

In the context of a single sermon, then, we want to help our hearers experience a sliver of their real guilt, but this experience is neither an end unto itself nor a direct means to action. Guilt rarely motivates good on its own. If acknowledging a problem is the first step to addressing it, a sermon must acknowledge our guilt in order to help the congregation be delivered from it. If hearers do not experience guilt, they cannot experience the joy of repentance. And if they do not repent, it is doubtful that they will eventually act individually and corporately in any more ethical fashion than they did before they heard the sermon. *Show* the congregation the way that others suffer and our relationship to that suffering, and they will repent and desire to follow a new path of treating others as Thous instead of Its.

That said, we must be careful not to show the congregation our sin in the vertical dimension in such vivid and incriminating fashion that the feeling of guilt becomes so overwhelming that hearers are unable to be delivered from it and envision this new path. This is why a cumulative approach to the human condition is so important for the pulpit. We should not only deal with little sins, but in an individual sermon we should deal with a little bit of sin *so that* our hearers can experience a little bit of grace leading to a little bit of new behavior.

That *new behavior* is the third element that must be shown. Too often we preachers show the problem and then just tell the congregation what to do about it.[8] As with making people feel guilty, telling people what to do rarely instills in them a desire to do it. They may recognize a need and/or a responsibility, but they will not feel a passion about it. Moreover, in today's world, many hearers will be skeptical about whether they are capable of doing what we preachers call them to do. Yes, they can act in more ethical ways toward their individual neighbors; but when we deal with broader issues of structural sin, our hearers feel overwhelmed. In today's global-

---

8. In a similar fashion, David L. Bartlett does an excellent job describing how preachers show sin but only tell mercy in "Showing Mercy" in *What's the Matter with Preaching Today?* (Louisville: Westminster John Knox, 2004), 37–50.

ized, twenty-four-hour newscast world, the problems of the world seem so large and persistent that we are overwhelmed. Preachers, I think, too often assume the inaction of our congregations is due to apathy. There may be some truth to this, but I think it is less the case than we think. I tend to believe that our hearers are generally concerned with the latest health crisis in Africa, heterosexism in our legislatures, terrorism in the Middle East, poverty in our city streets, potential war in Eastern Europe, racism in our police forces, deforestation in South America, and patriarchy in our denomination. They care about such issues, but they do not believe they can have an impact on them. The problems simply seem too massive for an individual or a community of faith to change. If we show them that they have a hand in being responsible for such situations and then tell them to do something about it, they will simply feel bad about the situation and bad about themselves. We must *show* the congregation ways others have made an impact on situations created by systemic sin to inspire in them a passion to act.

But this is difficult. Very difficult. So preachers often do homiletically what churches have done in terms of mission. The church often substitutes charity for acts of striving to transform the world. (While charity is a worthy element of the church's mission in terms of outreach to the suffering, it should not be the whole of that mission.) Homiletically, this translates into a sentimentality for individual acts of charity supported with imagery like the clichéd starfish story in which someone (usually told as a little girl with doe eyes) is casting a few starfish from the beach into the ocean before they die in the sun. When someone else asks what difference it makes when there are hundreds of other starfish lying in the sun that will die, the little girl justifies her actions by looking at the one in her hand and saying, "It makes a difference to this one," as she casts it back into the sea. Such a story is sure to evoke warm hearts and teary eyes, but at some point some astute person in the pew will (or should!) raise her hand and ask, "Is that it? Sure, saving the few starfish makes the girl feel good and makes the few starfish who have been saved feel good, if starfish feel anything. But what about the other hundreds of starfish who die of dehydration on the beach? Wouldn't the girl have done better to organize a brigade of volunteers to get all of the starfish back into the water? Sure, we feel great after working in a soup kitchen on Thanksgiving, and, yes, those who are fed receive a blessing. But what about the 20,000+ people who die every day from starvation? Is 'It makes a difference to this one' all we've got as a church?"

Of course, preachers must be realistic. We will certainly always have the poor with us (since the human condition is persistent), and we should not try to paint a picture of the results of ethical action that is a fictional utopia. But neither should we aim too small, in a way that makes both the issues of the world and the Christian response to them seem insignificant. As we must look at the results of our sins with honesty, we must imagine what can be done with an equal mix of realism and hope.

Preachers, therefore, must show the church a reflection of itself that makes a real and broad difference in the world. In other words, we should preach a mixture of eschatology and ontology instead of exhortation. By eschatology, I mean we envision the world as it might be in contrast to how it is.[9] Christ's preaching that uses the metaphor of the reign of Christ is a model for doing this. The reign of heaven is to be understood over against the reign of this world (especially the reign of Caesar), and thus is a thoroughly political concept; but it is also more than a political reference alone. Jesus never defines the reign of heaven, but only describes it in parables that evoke questions about one's relation to the reign of heaven more than answering questions about the nature of God's reign itself. A new order has begun in Christ. But this new order is not complete. Even though the reign of heaven has approached, the church is to pray for its coming. Preachers do well to interpret this biblical theme in experiential

9. The following discussion of eschatology grows out of a discussion of the theme in relation to the Gospel of Matthew in O. Wesley Allen, Jr., *Matthew*, Fortress Biblical Preaching Commentaries (Minneapolis, Fortress, 2013), 19–22.

terms instead of chronological ones. Eschatological existence can be compared to driving a car on a lonely country road (with no street lamps) at night. With no oncoming traffic, you put your high-beam lights on and ease toward the center of the road a little. But then as you begin to rise up a slope, you see headlight beams coming from the other side of the hill. You move back to the right some and turn off the high beams. This is a simplified version of already/not-yet. You have not yet met the vehicle coming your way, but you have already adjusted your driving in relation to its approach. To be a Christian shaped by the Christ event but living in a world shaped also by evil forces in which we sinfully participate is to live every day with the headlights but not the full reality of the vehicle. This is the eschatological element of preaching about the vertical dimension of the human condition. We preach the vision of a just and peaceful world that we help create but which is not yet because we have already experienced God's justice and peace offered to the world in Christ.

Conversely, by ontology I mean that we show our hearers the nature of the Christian life individually and the church corporately *as it is theologically speaking* instead of calling it to be something it is not yet. We are well aware the church is filled with wheat and tares; but having presented our sinful responsibility for the suffering of our neighbors earlier in the sermon, in the good-news portion of the sermon we offer the congregation wheat. In the creed we profess to believe in the church in the same breath and using the same language that we believe in the Triune God. This is the church ontologically speaking. This is the church (and its members) that we proclaim in our sermons. In other words, we show our hearers the Christian life and the church as God has defined instead of as we have corrupted it. In this way, hearers are inspired to live into who we are as opposed to trying to overcome who we are not.

Sample Sermon

The following sermon from a number of years ago is on the familiar passage from Micah 6:1-8. It is known mainly for verse 8:

"He has told you, human one, what is good and the Lord requires from you: to do justice, embrace faithful love, and walk humbly with your God." Too often, however, the quote is used as a proof text without knowledge of the context in which it arises. The sermon attempts to take the setting of a trial scene seriously to convict hearers of our sinfulness while moving beyond this conviction to a vision of ethical action that brings about true change.

We Americans love a good trial. We watch courtroom dramas on TV: *Perry Mason, Matlock, LA Law, The Practice, Boston Legal*. We watch them at the theaters: *To Kill a Mockingbird, Twelve Angry Men, Erin Brockovich, A Few Good Men*, and all 750 John Grisham movies. Trials entertain us.

But not just fictional trials. Real-life trials entertain us too, although we might not be comfortable admitting that. Michael Jackson, Scott Peterson, Kobe Bryant, Bill Clinton, O. J. Simpson, Leopold and Loeb, the Lindberg kidnapper. Heck, we even have Court TV that treats trials like sports events with play-by-play commentary and trial round-ups throughout the day. Those trials aren't enough, so we create *The People's Court*, Judge Judy, Judge Mathis, Judge Mills Lane, Judge Joe Brown, and Judge Hatchett. Trials entertain us.

Of course, sometimes trials grab us in a way that moves us beyond entertainment. Sometimes, even though we're observers, trials make us question our core values and our very understanding of what is right and wrong in the world: Watergate, *Brown v. the Board of Education*, Nuremburg, Scopes Monkey Trial, Amistad, the trial of Galileo, the trial of Jesus. Trials move us, challenge us, call us to question who we are and to change what we do.

And today's lesson from Micah is just such a trial that we can observe. The text opens with the bailiff calling the court to order and inviting the two parties forward to argue their cases before the jury: "Hear what the Lord is saying:

Arise, lay out the lawsuit before the mountains; let the hills hear your voice!" (6:1). The mountains are the jury? Why mountains? The reasoning is clear in the bailiff's instruction to the jury: "Hear, mountains, the lawsuit of the Lord! Hear, eternal foundations of the earth! The Lord has a lawsuit against his people; with Israel he will argue" (v. 2). Since the participants in the case are God and God's people, the mountains are the perfect jury—with their foundation on earth and their peaks stretching up to the heavens, who could better serve as mediators between the human and the divine?

The court has been called to order, the jury instructed, and now the plaintiff steps up to offer an opening statement. It is God who is suing Israel:

> O my people, what have I done to you?
> > In what have I wearied you? Answer me!
> For I brought you up from the land of Egypt,
> > and redeemed you from the house of slavery;
> and I sent before you Moses,
> > Aaron, and Miriam.
> O my people, remember now what King Balak of Moab
> > devised,
> > what Balaam son of Beor answered him,
> and what happened from Shittim to Gilgal,
> > that you may know the saving acts of the Lord.
> > (vv. 3-5)

It is a breach-of-contract case. God presents evidence to show that there is no fault on the divine side of the covenant. "Didn't I rescue you from Egypt? Didn't I bring you into the promised land and protect you from armies posed against you?" What comes next is not stated, but it's not stated loudly: "I kept my side of the contract, but the people have not lived up to theirs."

Then the lawyer for the defense stands up and declares to the mountains with as much sarcasm as humanity can muster that Israel has lived up to the human side of the contract. It's just that God is a jealous, greedy God who always wants more:

> With what should I approach the Lord
> > and bow down before God on high?
> Should I come before him with entirely burned offerings,
> > with year-old calves?
> Will the Lord be pleased with thousands of rams,
> > with many torrents of oil?
> Should I give my oldest child for my crime;
> > the fruit of my body for the sin of my spirit?
> (vv. 6-7)

It doesn't take the jury of mountains long to deliberate. They pronounce their judgment against the defendant:

> He has told you, human one, what is good and
> > what the LORD requires from you:
> > > to do justice, embrace faithful love, and walk
> humbly with your God. (v. 8)

Now some of my students worry that too much of seminary is abstract. They're always on the lookout for things that are immediately useful, and when they hear it in class, they'll say, "That'll preach!" As I studied this text it became clear to me that this was that sort of text. It'll Preach! with a capital *P* and an exclamation point. And let me tell you, I was ready to do just that. I was ready to preach this text. I was ready to let Micah loose on the extreme Christian right who claim to have cornered the market on "moral values" but fail to invest anything more than pocket change in social ethics.

But then, darn it, I made the mistake that other students of mine make in the middle of preparing a sermon: I talked to a seminary professor about what I was doing. It was Dr. Lisa Davison,[10] who teaches Bible. And she took a perfectly simple, straightforward idea and made it complicated. I told her about this sermon on Micah 6 that I was working on—mind you, I'm just making small

---

10. Lisa Davison, conversation with the author, January 20, 2005.

talk, just giving information, not seeking advice, but that never stopped a seminary professor from putting in his or her own four cents. I told her I was working on Micah 6, and she said, "Oh, that's a great text, but I think all the translations have it wrong. It's not that God demands us "to do justice, and to love kindness, and to walk humbly with your God" [NRSV]. The Hebrew is stronger than that. A better translation is that God requires us "to make justice happen, to love passionately as God loves, and to remember that, although we are not God, we are God's very own." Suddenly, I began asking myself, "Hey! Who's on trial here? I'm supposed to be an observer of this trial!" I wanted to lament other Christians that I don't think share my level of concern for justice, only to hear in this translation that being concerned for justice ain't enough. I mean, there's a huge difference between "doing justice" and "making justice happen." It's one thing to live your individual life justly—to be honest in business dealings, to volunteer in a homeless shelter, to treat people as equals regardless of who they are. Those things are good, but they're not the same thing as making justice happen. They're not the same thing as taking our corrupt systems in society and making them just. Who's on trial here?

When I was dean of the chapel at DePauw University, I admired the students who were most active in trying to bring about social changes for the better but didn't participate in religious life activities on campus at all. These were the students who led teach-ins about sweatshops making all the clothes we buy in the college bookstore and Wal-Mart and from Kathy Lee and Michael Jordan. These are the young men and women who traveled from Indiana to Georgia to protest at the School of the Americas our taxes pay for. These were the students who protested outside the administration building with tape over their mouths to force the university president to issue a statement following the violent death of Matthew Shepherd. These were the students who negotiated with the university's board of trustees to secure that at least a portion of the school's endowment be assigned to socially responsible investments. And these were the students who never darkened the door of the church. When I asked them why that was, they said they didn't see church as relevant for society anymore. They said the church had sold its soul in order to make people in the pews feel better about themselves instead of making the world a better place for all. And I, the chaplain, said to them, "Hey! Who's on trial here?"

It's me . . . "It's me, it's me, O Lord, standing in the need of prayer." It's me on trial here. I'm a nice, decent person, but this text from Micah says that God requires more than decency, indeed that God requires more of us than just being concerned about justice. I have been told that Stanley Hauerwas used to accuse our denomination [United Methodism] of having only one doctrine: "God is nice, therefore you should be nice too." That's bad theology. But it's even worse ethics. Being concerned about justice is nice, but nobody changed the world to look more like God's reign by being nice. Being nice is to be an accomplice to injustice. But God stands before the jury and says the church is not to be an accomplice to suffering. God says the church is not nice. God says, the church makes justice happen.

A couple of years ago, I went to Memphis for an academic conference, and one of the things the organizers had planned for us was a visit to the National Civil Rights Museum. It's housed in the Loraine Motel. As you walk through the winding hallways of the museum, you see photos of protests in Berkley, California, you push buttons and hear recordings of great speeches and loud spirituals, you read "White only" signs, and you stand where Dr. Martin Luther King Jr. fell when he was shot.

And at one point in the tour, you get to walk into an old restored bus from Montgomery, Alabama. Holding on to that cold, metal rail and climbing up those rubber-padded steps at the front of the bus, I was filled with pride and shame at the same time. Being there seemed an appropriate way to honor those African Americans who boycotted the bus system a little over fifty years ago in my home state. And when I had stepped all the way in and looked back into the bus, I saw a sign inviting you to sit at the very row where Rosa Parks sat on the bus when she refused to "move on back." When I sat down, there was sort of a familiar feel to the seat. A little uncomfortable, but familiar. But I couldn't quite put my finger on what the seat felt like; I just knew that I'd felt that kind of seat before.

Anyway, I sat there in that ordinary, smelly ol' bus and noticed a button you can push. There are buttons all over the museum that start recordings about this or that. So I pushed this one expecting to hear a narration about Rosa Parks and the boycott. But instead a voice from the front of the bus somewhat politely (only somewhat) told me to move to the back of the bus to make room for others who are getting on. A second later the voice was louder, angrier, full of disrespect and hatred, ordering me to get to the back. Another second later the voice is shouting and threatening that if I do not move now the police will be called and cart my sorry carcass off to jail.

And sitting there, in that museum bus, with nothing but a tape recording yelling at me yet with that bus somehow echoing with the cries of generations of oppressed and suffering brothers and sisters, I understood the difference between "doing justice" and "making justice happen." And at that moment I remembered what that uncomfortable bus seat felt like—it felt just a little bit like a church pew.

Suffering

Theological

Having examined the task of preaching in relation to the broken relationship between human and human from the side of our sin causing our neighbors to suffer, we turn now to the other side of the relationship—when we are victims of others' sinfulness. As we are all sinners in this horizontal, ethical sense of sin, we are all also victims of ethical wrongs. We all suffer in the horizontal dimension of the human condition. If you are human, you have been hurt by other humans.

We, of course, are not all victims of such injury to the same degree. Everyone experiences individual insult and pain in life, but some experience severe physical and emotional abuse at the hands of "loved ones" that others cannot imagine. Moreover, while all suffer at the individual level, we do not all suffer from systemic oppression caused by a collective of others. I am a white, Euro-American, middle-class, middle-aged, educated, heterosexual, able-bodied male. I am the very picture of contemporary privilege. The most that has ever happened to me simply due to who I am is to have people make fun of my height, weight, or Southern accent—and most of these instances were not done to harm me but to laugh with me. I have never been the target of structural racism, classicism, ageism, heterosexism, ableism, or sexism. I would certainly argue that those who participate intentionally or unintentionally in the systemic oppression of others are made less than we can be alongside the victims on the underside of oppression, but not in any way to the same degree or in the same manner that those whose physical, psychological, economic, social, material, and spiritual well-being are threatened, damaged, or utterly destroyed simply because of who they are or where or when they were born.

Preaching to a congregation that has experienced and/or continues to experience systemic marginalization versus preaching to one shaped by social privilege will require of preachers different cumulative strategies. Nevertheless, preachers must be careful not to preach only sermons dealing with our sinfulness in the horizontal dimension to privileged congregations and only sermons dealing with suffering to those who have been oppressed. While not equally, all have sinned on the ethical plane and all have suffered on it—all of us have been treated as Its instead of Thous at different times in our lives. To address the full human condition over time in a congregation, the injuries caused by such It-ifying by others should be appropriately named in relation to the varied experiences of those in the pews.

Of course, theologians and preachers offer a range of interpretations of God's good news in relation to suffering at the hands of others, especially given the fact that ethics have been central in modern and postmodern theology and pastoral care has played such an important role in preaching in the twentieth century and beyond. In relation to theology, God is lifted up as the liberator of those who suffer from structural oppression and marginalization. In terms of pastoral care, God as the omnipresent Comforter is emphasized. In both, the church is emphasized as an agent of God's concern for the suffering, a community of solace and activism transforming individual lives and the world more broadly, alleviating suffering wherever the church encounters it.

Biblical

The Hebrew Bible is filled with texts that exemplify these three concerns (God as liberator, God as comforter, and the community of faith as a place of care for the suffering). The ethical commands discussed earlier in the section on sin show God is concerned with victims of unloving, unmerciful, and unjust behavior and structures. These instructions especially call the people of Israel and Judah to be a community that cares for the widow and the orphan, the oppressed and downtrodden. The psalms, especially the individual laments, are filled with expressions professing faith in God's care for those who suffer at the hands of others, as are narratives presenting

God as rescuing someone who is in a situation of distress brought on by others.

Of course, the central story of Hebrew canon that relates to this dimension of the human condition is that of the exodus. God challenges Pharaoh, liberates the Israelites from slavery in Egypt, cares for their basic needs in their journey in the wilderness, and instructs the community's leadership in care of the people.

In the New Testament, this characterization of God and the community of faith as caring for those wronged by others continues on especially in the portrayal of the Christ event. The God who liberates the Israelites from slavery is also the God who liberates Jesus from the tomb.

Christ suffers as we suffer, and his redemption from death points toward our liberation as well. Tradition does not present Christ as dying a peaceful death in his sleep as an old man but as one murdered by a militaristic regime in conjunction with socio-religious leaders seeking to protect their status quo. Christ's suffering, death, and resurrection are political in that they expose the powerlessness of oppressive, corrupt exertions of power. This good news must be expressed, however, in eschatological fashion. God's resurrecting, liberating reign has already come in Jesus Christ, but any quick glance at the continued state of the world shows it is yet to be consummated. We must be honest that Caesar and his Pontius Pilates are alive and well without turning to despair or apathy as if we had not heard that on the third day God raised up Christ from the grave in which Pilate placed him.

Not only Christ's death and resurrection, but Christ's teaching is also relevant to preaching in relation to the horizontal dimension of the human condition. Christ teaches about reconciliation. Christians who are persecuted and suffer at the hands of others are expected to forgive. But this is not cheap grace that Jesus proclaims. For example, in his ecclesiological discourse, Matthew presents Jesus as calling Peter to forgive seven (or seventy) times seven times, but only after naming a process by which the church expels someone who refuses to right a wrong they have done to another member of the community of faith (Matt 18:15-22). Being wronged is not something Jesus takes lightly.

Homiletical

When we preach on sin in relation to ethics toward others, we have to convince our hearers of their sinfulness, especially in relation to broader structures of oppression. But when preaching on the suffering side of this dimension, no convincing is needed. All are aware that they have pain in their lives caused by others. When the preacher mentions brokenness in individual relationships, being looked down on by others for various reasons, words that have stung, and inequitable treatment at school or work, all will be nodding their heads. When the sermon offered to a marginalized community speaks of economic disparity, disregard for personhood, lack of a voice in society, and fear of private and public retaliation for desiring the same rights as others, the sanctuary will be filled with Amens.

There is, however, a difference between recognizing that we suffer and feeling that naming that fact has a place in faith and worship. We must turn the other cheek, after all. But as any psychotherapist knows, emotional healing of one who has been hurt rarely comes without a patient being able to name honestly what has been done to them. Rephrased in theological terms, we can say that reconciliation and forgiveness require a naming of what needs to be forgiven.

This has become a basic tenet of restorative justice. In prisons, victims and offenders are brought into frank and painful conversation so that both might find healing. The Truth and Reconciliation Commission in South Africa after the fall of apartheid was a great witness to the power of naming ways others have sinned against us in order to move beyond those injuries. The preacher must model for and give permission to hearers to lift up ways they have been wronged by others in a similar fashion. The pulpit is not the place for therapy or full-blown exposure of one's wounds. But it is the place for naming injuries in ways that can fund more detailed work at other times.

We should show the bandages but perhaps not rip them off completely. Naming wounds honestly in a sermon leads to healing. Too much exposure can raise up more pain than can be dealt with in the time limits of a sermon and end up causing more pain than good.

In naming injuries we and our hearers have experienced, we must also be careful not to demonize those who have sinned against us. We are not arbiters of their standing before God. More than that, as we have acknowledged above, we have all sinned against our neighbors and most have participated, directly or indirectly, in some form of structural oppression of others. Thus, even while our homiletical focus is on suffering experienced by those in worship, we should have a tone of empathy for those who cause such suffering. Empathy does not mean releasing offenders from responsibility for the harm they have done; it simply means that we are concerned for their well-being as well. Those who injure and those who are injured are both trapped in the human condition.

The purpose of preaching on our suffering at the hands of others, then, is not to lay blame on the offenders nor to tell the injured to "get over it." It is to help hearers experience God's reconciling love in relation to pain they have experienced in a way that offers hope for that reconciliation to be effected in human affairs and empowerment in addressing the pain experienced. Thus we preachers must show our congregations the potential and power of reconciliation as honestly as we have shown our suffering. We must offer examples of people who, through God's grace, have struggled with and overcome pain inflicted by others. We must show communities who have fought and continue to fight against ways in which they are systemically victimized as part of their understanding of their Christian vocation. In a word, then, after having named particular ways in which our hearers experience suffering at the hands of others, we need to offer a vision of what it means to be lovingly and powerfully defined by God in the face of that suffering instead of being defined by the suffering itself.

Sample Sermon

For all the joy and hope the celebration of the Nativity offers to Christians, the secular emphasis on family gatherings and gift giving leads to the season being painful for many. Knowing that everyone else at school will be talking about what Santa brought them when you got nothing is painful. Being gay and having to visit family apart from your partner because he or she will never be welcomed there is painful. Being given processed turkey and dressing at the local shelter and then spending the rest of Christmas on the street is painful. Being single during the holidays after a series of painful divorce hearings in which horrific accusations were made is painful. Christmas joy experienced by others can be salt in the wound for those already suffering.

The following sermon on Matthew 2:13-23, Herod's slaughter of the Innocents innocents following news of Jesus's birth, was preached on the Sunday after Christmas and was intended to recognize such suffering.[11] It is in the form of a story-sermon, in which the entire sermon is a fictional narrative intending to convey gospel truth. This technique invites hearers to identify with "Maxie" in the story—an identification that occurs in a way that allows hearers to acknowledge their own suffering in a safe distance if they need to do so.

> Maxie Johnston had the voice of a Siren. And it worked its magic on me, because I would go down to her house to sing with her every chance I got when I was a child. Her tiny farm was about three miles outside of Tinyville, and I would sprint the whole way.
>
> Whenever I came to her door, we went through this ritual:
>
>> I'd step up on the porch and listen for singing inside. Then I would knock three times slowly. [Knock three times on the pulpit.]

---

11. This sermon was originally published in O. Wesley Allen, Jr., *Good News from Tinyville: Stories of Heart and Hope* (St. Louis: Chalice, 1999), 55–59. The version here has been altered slightly.

[Mimic the opening of a door.] She'd open the door and say, "Why, Jackson Hillman! Whatever brings you all the way out here?"

"Well, Miss Johnston," I would answer, "I was wondering if you might be in a singing mood today."

"Look, I told you to call me Maxie, and you know that I'm always in a singing mood! You just come on in and bring your little voice with you."

Then we'd go inside and sing. Of course, we'd only sing hymns. Maxie didn't believe in any other kind of music. She would always say that when we sang hymns, we came the closest we could to being angels on earth.

And we'd only sing while we worked. She said that singing hymns while we worked changed our chores into kingdom work. Even at nine years old I knew that was a trick to get me to help her with the farm work. But I didn't mind. I would have even done work at my own house to get to hear her voice.

Well, we'd start to work and she always chose hymns that had an appropriate tempo for whatever chore we were doing. When we swept we'd sing something like "Blessed Assurance, Jesus Is Mine." When we kneaded dough, we'd sing something slower like "Amazing Grace! How Sweet the Sound." And when we milked the cow or churned the butter, we sang songs with a strong beat [mimic milking and sing]:

> Onward, Christian Soldiers, marching as to war,
> With the cross of Jesus going on before.

She would only stop working and singing to tell the story behind a hymn. Maxie took great pride in knowing where different hymns came from. She'd say something like, "Jackson, did you know that 'Onward, Christian Soldiers' was written in England in the 1860s to be sung by children as they marched from one village to another during Pentecost?" Then, without taking a full breath, Maxie would start singing the next hymn and move on to the next chore.

Maxie's favorite time of the year was Christmas. She said everybody sang hymns while they worked during Christmas. And, of course, I always went over to sing them with *her*. When we swept [mimic sweeping and sing]:

> Away in a manger, no crib for his bed,
> the little Lord Jesus laid down his sweet head . . .

When we kneaded dough [mimic kneading and sing]:

> What child is this, who, laid to rest,
> On Mary's lap is sleeping?

When we milked [mimic milking and sing]:

> Angels we have heard on high
>   sweetly singing o'er the plains,
> and the mountains in reply
>   echoing their joyous strains.
> Gloria in excelsis Deo.
> Gloria in excelsis Deo.

"Jackson, did you know that 'Gloria in excelsis Deo' was the first Christmas carol ever sung? Right after Jesus was born some angels appeared to a group of shepherds and sang it. When we sing it we ought to sing louder than we sing any other song, because when we sing it, we're singing the angels' song!"

"I don't understand," I said. "Why did the angels sing about 'egg shells'?"

Maxie laughed at me and answered, "No, no, Jackson. You see, angels only know how to sing in Latin. 'Gloria in excelsis Deo' is Latin for 'Glory to God in the highest'!" *That* was the first Christmas carol ever sung."

I'm not sure if I was trying to catch Maxie with some piece of hymn trivia she didn't know, or if I was just in an especially inquisitive mood, but before she could get back to work, I piped up and asked her, "Maxie, what was the *second* Christmas carol ever sung?"

Suddenly Maxie got a very serious look on her face and pulled me up into her lap as she sat there on that milking stool. She started, "It's a song we rarely sing anymore; but everyone who lives in this old world knows its words by heart and keeps its tune locked up in their soul. [Pause.]

"You know the story of the magi coming from the east to worship Jesus when he was born? Well, ol' Herod was one mad king when he found out that they had returned to the east without telling him where in Bethlehem they had found the child-king that they were searching for. So mad that he ordered his army to kill every boy in and around Bethlehem who was two years old or younger. That way he'd make sure that there was no newborn king around to steal his throne . . . or at least that's what he thought.

"What could be said to a village that had bloodshed in so many of its homes? What could be said to a community that would go two years without a single *bar mitzphah*? What could be said to comfort the parents of all those innocent babies that had been murdered, all because Herod had wanted to kill Jesus? Nothing. Nothing could be said. No speech could make the pain disappear.

"But someone did remember a song that would give expression to their pain. It was a song, written by Jeremiah the prophet hundreds of year earlier. The song tells about Rachel, who was considered the mother of the northern tribes of Israel, weeping from inside her tomb located at Ramah, weeping because of the death and exile of all her children. When it was sung in Bethlehem that bloody day, it became the second Christmas carol ever sung:

> A voice was heard in Ramah,
>> weeping and much grieving.
> Rachel weeping for her children,
>> and she did not want to be comforted,
>> because they were no more."

As a nine-year-old I didn't know a lot about death or injustice, but I thought I knew Christmas. And I said, "Maxie, that story can't be right. Christmas is about presents and laughter and birth."

She said, "Well, you know, Jackson, all the suffering in the world doesn't stop just because it's Christmas. But, you're right, Christmas is about more than the story of Herod slaughtering the innocents. It's about the rest of the story as well. You see, what Herod didn't know was that the same angel that had told the magi to go home without speaking to Herod told Joseph to take Mary and Jesus and high-tail it out of Bethlehem to Egypt until Herod died. So no matter how much destruction Herod could cause, he couldn't stop the work God was starting to do through Jesus. After all, if a tomb couldn't stop Jesus, Herod wasn't going to be able to do it."

I thought about everything she had told me for a minute while she just held me on her lap. Finally I said, "But if Herod died, why do we ever need to sing that Christmas carol again?"

"Well," Maxie said as she sniffed just a little bit, "after Herod died, Joseph brought the family back home to Bethlehem. But when they got there, they found out that Herod Jr. had taken his daddy's place on the throne. So they had to move to Nazareth to be safe from him. You see, there always have been and always will be Herods around trying to stop God from being with the world. Of course, they're never successful. And that's why we celebrate Christmas and why it's fun. But as long as they keep trying, there's going to be pain in the world too. And we need to keep singing that second Christmas carol for the people who are suffering from one thing or another, and we need to remember that God is with them in a special way."

The three-mile walk home that day seemed longer than ever. For the first time I began to wonder why Maxie had never married and had never spoken about any family. I wondered why she only had one cow and why her house was so small. I wondered why I helped her make bread a lot, but never helped her cook a chicken. I wondered why she always teared up when we sang "Abide with Me." I wondered why any time I talked about my daddy, she touched the scar on her cheek. And I wondered why I only ever saw her in two dresses—one for work and one for church. I never asked her any of those questions. But as I spent more time with Maxie, I came to realize why I liked being with her so much: because God was with her in a special way.

For me Christmas will always contain thoughts of Maxie Johnston. She was the angel who taught me that Christ *is* born. And because of her I will always sing "Gloria in excelsis Deo" a little louder than all of the other Christmas carols. And then I will always pause afterward . . . to remember the second Christmas carol ever sung.

THE INNER DIMENSION OF THE HUMAN CONDITION

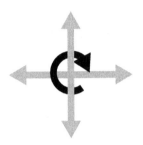

Our overarching concern in this book is with the preacher's task of proclaiming how God's good news addresses the human condition, that is, the threats and damage done to the physical, intellectual, psychological, spiritual, material, and social well-being of human beings individually and human communities collectively. We are using the greatest commandment—"You must love the Lord your God with all your heart, with all your being, with all your mind, and with all your strength. . . . You will love your neighbor as yourself" (Mark 12:30-31)—as a heuristic lens through which to view and bring the three dimensions of the human condition into a cumulative homiletical approach.

In this chapter, we are focusing specifically on the inner dimension of the human condition implied in the command to your neighbor *as yourself*. While the text is not concerned with self-love, the language of loving another as we love ourselves evokes concern about the relationship between a person and him- or herself. There is brokenness internal to the human being that threatens and damages our well-being. Because it is internal, sin and suffering collapse upon one another—we sin against ourselves, causing our own suffering. This inner dimension of our model of the human condition focuses on the psyche of the human being.

Brokenness in the inner dimension of the human being is the usual starting point for dealing with the human condition by theologians and preachers in various strands of liberal theology who claim an individualistic approach to anthropology as the best starting point for doing theology—for example, existentialist, some process, and some revisionist theologies. It is also strongly emphasized (even if not the theological starting point) by evangelicals, Pentecostals, and those in pietistic traditions at the other end of the theological spectrum, who have traditionally placed a high priority on the conversion and transformation of individuals. There is a good rationale behind emphasizing this dimension in that it builds on psychological understandings of humanity that arose during the twentieth century matched with concerns for the spiritual transformation and care of the soul of individuals in scripture, tradition, and Christian practice.

For preachers who hold the inner dimension as primary for understanding the human condition, the vertical and horizontal dimensions are seen as derivative of the vertical. In other words, if the core problem of the human condition is seen as internal brokenness, then this brokenness in turn causes brokenness in relationships between humanity and God and in the relationships of humans with humans. Conversely, for those who hold that either of the other two dimensions are primary for understanding the human condition theologically, the inner dimension is seen as resulting from either brokenness in the relationship with the Divine or brokenness in the ethical dimension.

Regardless of where one starts, however, any description of the human condition or cumulative preaching that fails to deal adequately with sin and suffering in the inner dimension offers only a partial and thus a flawed understanding of the situation in which we humans exist. After all, a broken relationship with oneself causes damage to our other relationships, with God and neighbor. It is difficult to love others when we cannot love ourselves. And our internal pain is inseparable from the questions we have about God's relationship to suffering and pain inflicted on us by our fellow human beings. When we place idols before God, we make both the One who deserves our worship and the one doing the worshipping small. When we treat others as Its (objects to be consumed) instead of Thous (subjects with whom to be in mutually beneficial relationships), we turn ourselves into Its.

Of course, thinkers in the different schools who start with this dimension cannot be reduced to similarities in all the ways they approach the inner dimension of the human condition. For example, they approach the role of God in very different ways. Some view God as an active spiritual presence in the lives of individuals in ways that transform and sanctify them, leading to self-fulfillment. Others argue such traditional theological language is metaphorical, indicating that God is the Ground of Being, the one (or that) which gives meaning to our existence, which leads to self-fulfillment.

Still, in one way or another, whether understood literally or figuratively, scholars and preachers dealing with this dimension of the human condition lift up God as the one who creates us with a purpose and redeems us so that we might experience and fulfill that meaning for our lives and find well-being in that meaning. God is holy, demanding that we be holy and making us to be holy.

Expressed conversely from the human side, theology and sermons focusing on the inner dimension recognize that humans have distorted and denied the fact that we have been made in the *imago Dei*, and we cannot reclaim it on our own. We are dependent on God for converting us for the sake of our own well-being. We are dependent on God to establish the meaning of life, the meaning of our individual lives. We are dependent on God for sanctification and the emotional and spiritual well-being that comes from it. In other words, everything that humans do is in response to God's initiative in prescribing meaning for our existence, whether we recognize it or not. God calls us to our full potential and we respond, individually, by deciding in favor of and acting in accordance with God's will for our lives or by selecting meaning for our individual lives that is actually counterproductive to our own best interests, leading to misplaced or unhealthy self-esteem. This inner dimension of the human condition, then, is really related to the theological category of vocation. I mean this not in the narrow sense of occupation, but in the broader sense of God's calling on our lives that is given to us for our own good. As it is stated in the United Methodist funeral ritual, "No mortal life [God has] made is without eternal meaning."[1]

Therefore, the internal relationship between a human and her- or himself can be said to be broken when, for various reasons, the divinely gifted, eternal meaning of an individual's finite existence is not fulfilled. It is the state of being estranged from one's true self by putting our life energy into propping up an inauthentic self. And because this dimension of the human condition is a psychological, existential state of being, the two sides of sin and suffering are not simply related in an inseparable fashion as in the other two dimensions; here they collapse in on one another, and must be treated together.

Sin and Suffering

Theological

We fail miserably in living up to our God-given purposes and having a sense of self-fulfillment in life. Humans suffer self-estrangement because we are finite *and* we are aware of our finitude. Our awareness of our mortality and other limitations causes fear and despair, leading to attempts to deny or overcome that

---

1. *The United Methodist Book of Worship* (Nashville: United Methodist Publishing House, 1992), 163.

mortality and limitation by claiming to be someone we cannot and should not be, which in turn leads to greater awareness of our finitude and greater attempts to negate it. This is not a situation in which we can choose not to participate. We cannot escape it by our own determination and actions. It is a cyclical state of being that can be described as sinful suffering. Our essence is good—that is, our essence of being made in God's image for good purposes in the world—but because our existence is limited, we fail to experience and live up to that good essence. Indeed, we actively resist living up to that good essence. We sin against ourselves, causing self-suffering.

We commit a wide range of sinful actions against ourselves that cause and grow out of internal suffering—that is, we do damage to our own psyches in diverse ways. We have many ways in which we feel inadequate and take many missteps in dealing with the feelings. We look for self-worth in all the wrong places. In various situations and relationships we take actions that we convince ourselves is for our own good, but that in truth lead to self-destruction to different degrees. We enter into or stay in unhealthy relationships in order to affirm that we are desirable as a family member, friend, or mate. We take employment that has the potential for economic advancement but which we experience daily as drudgery. We overspend hoping that having "stuff" will prove our worth. We silence our voice so that we might be affirmed by others, or we pontificate loudly not just to express our concern but to gain the respect of others in the form of having power over them. We sabotage our own opportunities for fulfillment, happiness, and peace. Self-doubt at one end of the spectrum and overconfidence at the other both lead us to isolation and self-hatred.

Yet all of these examples can be seen as symptoms of a single, inescapable condition. We lack appropriate self-esteem and self-care that is rooted in God's view, love, and hope for us and thus we turn to other ways of dealing with our self-image that are actually damaging to the self. The collapse of sin and suffering as a state of being in this inner dimension can be described with a contemporary metaphor—addiction. This metaphor can work with the other dimensions as well (or the whole of the human condition) but seems especially fitting for this one. Addiction to alcohol, drugs, eating patterns, sex, and so on are forms of (conscious or unconscious) self-medicating approaches to dealing with depression, anxiety, alienation, and the like. But one does not choose this approach. Addiction is a disease, a biological condition that leads to certain adverse behaviors, and those behaviors in turn make the condition worse. The addict is powerless over the condition but paradoxically must be empowered to take responsibility for the behaviors in order to manage the condition so that the addict can experience a state of recovery. Similarly, sin as an internal brokenness is an existential condition under which we suffer because of things we cannot help doing to ourselves and yet for which we must be empowered to take responsibility because we cannot take responsibility on our own. The human condition is one in which the world tells us that we are not good enough. We cannot help but internalize this message and act negatively upon ourselves because of it. We cannot pull ourselves out of this mire. But neither does God's gift of vocation—the best meaning and purpose of our unique, individual life—force us out of it. God empowers us to take responsibility for the meaning of our life in a way we cannot do alone.

In other words, our failure in terms of sinfully causing our own self-suffering is not the last word on the inner dimension of the human condition. Our sinful nature is answered by God's desire for our individual well-being. Whereas traditional language of atonement and reconciliation fit the other two dimensions in which we are related to others, metaphors of renewal, regeneration, new birth, new creation, and sanctification fit with this dimension in which we are related to ourselves. Salvation in relation to this dimension of the human condition is individual transformation through which we are brought closer to the God-gifted meaning of and potential for our lives and are enabled to make a decision to pursue authentic existence.

Biblical

The Hebrew Bible is filled with concern for such transformation of individuals. Nowhere is this more evident than in the moral code of Leviticus (as well as the ritual and legal sections) in which expectations of Israel being a holy people are codified. Even though the emphasis is expressed in corporate terms, the commandments deal with individual behavior that is viewed as destructive to one's calling to be holy. (This same dynamic is found in the New Testament in 1 Peter.) Similarly, the wisdom traditions, in which a practical holiness is prescribed, is concerned with the character of the individual human being. There are also the many stories in which biblical characters are given new names, representing God's transformative work in their personhood. The same is true with call stories where God overcomes an inherent shortcoming of prophets-to-be, raising them up to the vocation that defines them. Finally, the penitential psalms request forgiveness related to the broken relationship between human and God in the vertical dimension of the human condition, but also pray for transformation and curing of the soul.

The New Testament shares such a concern for the transformation of the individual life for the person's own good. The ministry, death, and resurrection of Christ reveals our potentiality. Jesus is tempted like us following his baptism; he calls us to ways of holiness, even to the point of commanding that we be perfect as God in heaven is perfect; he heals people of illnesses, representing an internal condition they cannot overcome on their own; he anguishes in the garden, representing both our angst in the face of death and offering to us the possibility of overcoming that anxiety in obedience to God's will for our lives; and he is risen from the dead, representing our eschatological potential for being transformed from a citizen of the realm of death to one in the realm of life.

Paul's descriptions of salvation in terms of reconciling humans to God and others cannot be separated from his view that through Christ God transforms the individual into a new creation, transferring us from being slaves to sin to being slaves to God. For Paul, this transformation is represented in baptism in which we participate in Christ's death, that is we are dead to sin, become "in Christ," receive the Holy Spirit, and are granted the hope of walking in the newness of life represented in Christ's resurrection. It is God's continuing and continual salvific work of sanctification that follows from the once-for-all salvific act of justification.

Homiletical

Part of good preaching often involves making our hearers feel bad *so that* we can then offer them good news that will impact and transform not only how they feel but how they understand and experience God's grace and purposes for the world. When preaching on the inner dimension of the human condition, however, the hearer already feels bad about her- or himself. One in ten people struggle with some form of addiction.[2] One in five people suffer from mental illness,[3] with a person attempting suicide in the United States every thirty-eight seconds.[4] Addiction and mental illnesses are biological diseases that need to be treated as such. That said, they are intimately related to—cyclically provoked by and provoking issues of poor self-understanding and self-esteem—suffering in the inner dimension. Our pews are filled with people struggling with their psychological and spiritual well-being. We do not need

2. "New Data Show Millions of Americans with Alcohol and Drug Addiction Could Benefit from Health Care R," Partnership for Drug-Free Kids, September 28, 2010, www.drugfree.org/new-data-show-millions-of-americans-with-alcohol-and-drug-addiction-could-benefit-from-health-care-r/.

3. "Mental Health Facts in America," National Alliance on Mental Illness, accessed August 10, 2016, http://www.nami.org/NAMI/media/NAMI-Media/Infographics/GeneralMHFacts.pdf.

4. "Suicide Statistics," Emory Cares 4 U, accessed August 10, 2016, www.emorycaresforyou.emory.edu/resources/suicidestatistics.html.

to make people feel bad about themselves to address inner sinful suffering—they already feel bad in and about themselves.

What they may be unaware of and unable to think through because of their pain, however, are the causes of their inner pain. No single sermon, of course, can touch on all the reasons why people hurt down deep in their souls, so over time in different sermons we must address many different sources of this type of pain. Often it comes from outside of us. That is, it is suffering inflicted in the vertical or horizontal dimensions, but we internalize it. We suffer due to illness or disaster; at first, in the vertical dimension, we ask, "Why me, O God?" but eventually start believing we deserve whatever has happened to us.

Likewise we suffer because of treatment of others in the horizontal dimension. Someone in the past broke up with us saying, "It's me, not you," but we "know" it is really us, that we are unlovable. Women are told they do not deserve the same pay for men doing the same job. Gay people are told they do not deserve the right to be in love and marry. An abused spouse wrongly believes she deserves what she gets because if that was not the case she would not be abused by her husband in the same way she was by her mother. Poor people are told that the American dream means any of them could get themselves out of the structural mire of poverty if they just wanted to enough and worked hard enough. Children at school are bullied for almost any reason at hand—looks, athletic ability, the neighborhood in which they live, how they wear their hair, who their friends are, something they do or refuse to do, or a picture posted online. Transgender people are called freaks and told to stay the way they were identified on their birth certificate. Individuals and culture tell us that because we are female, brown, short, not skinny enough, not smart enough, not pretty enough, not wealthy enough, not talented enough, not like "us" enough, we are not human enough. We hear such things in direct and indirect ways repeated enough for a long enough time that we cannot help but believe that we are less than those who are different from us.

Inner pain is also self-inflicted. Our hearers are often in denial about their own role in the cycle of inner sinful suffering. When people say something like, "When I look back on my life, I wouldn't change a thing," they are trying to affirm that the pains and mistakes of the past led them to where they are now and thus in retrospect profitable. But the saying also functions like, "Sticks and stones may break my bones, but words will never harm me." We say this *because* it is a lie and words really have harmed us. We say it to try to diminish the pain we feel. Likewise those who say they have no regrets are speaking a lie. A person with no regrets is a person who is brain-dead and soul-dead or has experienced serious memory loss. We claim we have no regrets as an attempt to claim power over and thus negate the power of those regrets. But we all have regrets that affect the state of our psyche. Everyone wishes she or he could have do-overs on some life choices, do-overs that might have changed the course of one's life. Many worry whether their tiny life has made much of a positive difference in this huge world at all. Some know that their lives have had more negative than positive impact on the world. Our regrets may well (and should) relate to our behavior in relation to how we have treated our neighbors—because damage done to others can linger in the soul long, long after our actions have receded into the past. Hateful words spoken to someone. Love lost because we dumped one person to date another. The auto accident that caused property damage and physical injury because we were texting. The failure to stand up to someone telling an offensive racist, ethnic, or sexist joke. Such things haunt us and keep our spirits more dimly lit than they ought to be for long periods of time, sometimes until death do us part.

Too many preachers turn to pop psychology and self-help approaches to deal with the inner dimension of the human condition. Pastors should always be ready to refer people in need to professional psychological help, and they can find thousands of self-help books on Amazon.com on their own. But we should avoid playing the role of Dr. Phil or motivational speaker in the pulpit. There is a radical difference between sermons that invite hearers into the transforming effects of the good news of Jesus Christ on the inner life of the individual and those that offer advice on enriching your marriage, seven steps to success in life, the Beatitudes' approach to better attitudes, the power of positive thinking, or the Bible-based approach to losing weight. People love these kinds of sermons—they resemble the some forty-five thousand self-help books available at any given time. Popularity, however, does not assure the message is of the gospel. We preachers do not offer advice to our hearers out of the fact that our lives are so well put together. In relation to the inner dimension, our task as preachers who also sinfully suffer in the inner dimension is to examine the dimension theologically and help hearers experience God addressing it with grace and purpose.

First, we must help our hearers escape the brainwashing they have received from the world that tells them they are "less than." This is best done by helping them develop a theological anthropology affirming they are made in the image of God. We do not pretend that everything they have done is pleasing to God—this would be to deny the other two dimensions of the human condition. But we do remind them, over and over again, that they are of God, that God created them on the sixth day and said, "Very good." There is nothing we have done nor anything we can do that can strip us of God's image. There is nothing, therefore, that can separate us from God's love including how others view us or how much we hate ourselves. Helping people see themselves as God "sees" them, ontologically speaking—that is, as they are at the core of their created beings—will help them connect their view of their self-worth with God's eternal view instead of with the temporal views of us flawed and finite beings.

Second, we must show our hearers glimpses of moments when God has empowered people to decide to live authentically instead of living as defined by negative and unhealthy forces in the world. These are moments of *kairos*. Whereas *chronos* is the passing of normal, everyday time, the Greek word *kairos* can mean "opportune time," or "the right time," and this is the way it is usually used theologically. In this sense, *kairos* is not linear time (history) or cyclical time (the passing of the seasons). It is a moment in *chronos* when the extraordinary is possible/happens. It is a juncture in time when the right decision can change the course of one's history. It is extraordinary time. It is God's eternal time invading human time. *Kairos* is ahistorical, eschatological even. Yet every moment, in some sense, holds potential for *kairos*. Whether in this small or huge moment we choose to be the one God made us and calls us to be, or we choose something less, something regrettable: that is what is at stake. Left to our own abilities and reasoning, we will almost always choose the less. But thankfully, we are never left to our own devices. God is present in every moment, calling us to the good, offering us the good. When we show our hearers imagery in which others have received God's gift by responding in a positive, healthy, and transforming way in a moment of *kairos*, we offer them that same gift from God.

Sample Sermon

The following sermon was preached on the First Sunday in Lent, and focused on the Gospel lection for the day, Matthew's version of Jesus's temptation (Matt 4:1-11). The liturgical occasion called for some instruction concerning the new season of the church calendar into which the church was entering because later in the liturgy, an invitation to the worshippers to take up a Lenten discipline was to be extended (reiterating the invitation from Ash Wednesday). The sermon attempts to get the hearers to view this practice as dealing with the core of their Christian identity and vocation. In other words, it reads the story of Jesus's temptation as a lens through which to view our struggles in the inner dimension of the human condition.

In *The Color Purple,*[5] Alice Walker presents a conversation between Celie and Shug that is worthy of the halls of Perkins School of Theology where I teach. The two women are walking through a field of purple flowers, and the beauty of the sight raises for them the issue of the nature of God. Shug suggests that God made the flowers so beautiful because more than anything, God loves admiration. When Celie asks her if that means that God is vain, Shug answers by saying, "Naw," she says, "Not vain, just wanting to share a good thing. I think it [makes] God [angry] if you walk by the color purple . . . somewhere and don't notice it."

Did you notice? The white of Christmas is ancient past. The green of Epiphany has been folded and hung in the closet. Purple has appeared in their place. It slipped in on Wednesday when we are usually only here for supper, so it might be easy to have gone unnoticed. And if I hadn't called your attention to it today, you'd still have forty days ahead of us to take notice. You see, Lent is all about taking notice.

But taking notice of what? That's the question. Surely it's more than just taking notice of God's gift of purple. It's taking notice of God's gift of . . . Well, maybe it's best to enter from the side door.

Lent began in the early church as a period of preparation for baptism of converts. These converts would study the Bible and the faith intensely, they would pray constantly, and they would fast rigorously. It was a time to test out whether you really wanted to be a Christian or not. Do I really believe this stuff? Do I really want to live this Christian life? It is supposed to be different from the way other people live, you know. When you have faith in Christ and live in Christ, your life in the world doesn't buy into all the rhetoric about what a good worldly life is all about. So Lent evolved as a period for converts to try on the clothes of the Christian and see how they fit for a

---

5. Alice Walker, *The Color Purple* (New York: Harcourt Brace Jovanovich, 1982), 178.

while before you decide to take that step on Easter and be baptized into wearing Christ forever. You know, in the early church they symbolized that by stripping naked before getting into the baptismal waters and then being clothed in a new white robe when they stepped out. Doing that in front of the whole church takes some guts, some real commitment. Maybe you ought to consider that whole naked thing next time someone is baptized here. Lent was a time for testing out whether you were ready for the kind of commitment and vulnerability it takes to be a Christian.

It's no wonder then that the early church used the story of Jesus's temptation as the lens for interpreting this trial period. One thing you might notice about the story is that Lent seems to get the order backward. We test out the faith before deciding to commit. But in the Gospels, Jesus is baptized and then has his faith tested. But let's be clear. In the story, Jesus isn't someone who is lost like Hansel and Gretel and accidentally stumbles upon Satan's gingerbread house out in the wilderness. Satan doesn't sing a Siren's song that seduces Jesus into coming out to the wilderness. No, indeed, the Holy Spirit comes upon Jesus after his baptism and then this very Spirit that has come from God, that is somehow God, *leads* Jesus into the wilderness to be tested by the devil. There is intentionality here. Jesus doesn't just happen to be tested when he is in the wilderness; he goes out there *in order to be tempted.* I mean, for heaven's sake, he fasts for forty days *so that* he will be tempted.

That's where it comes from, you know. Lenten discipline, that is. Modeled on Jesus fasting for forty days while being tempted by the devil. During Lent we abstain from something insignificant that we desire (chocolate, soft drinks, television) *so that* we will be tempted to desire it all the more. Lent is temptation practice, if you will. We take on small temptations to rehearse for times when serious temptation comes knocking at our door and rattling our windows. We take on small disciplines so that we are ready for those hard, trying times in life when only self-discipline can get us through. To use an image from my home country of Alabama, Lent is like intentionally letting yourself get bitten by mosquitoes *so that* you can practice resisting the temptation to scratch when you get a bad case of poison ivy. Notice I didn't say *if* you get a bad case of poison ivy. I said *when*. In Alabama, everyone stumbles into poison ivy now and then. It's everywhere. It's unavoidable. But if you scratch you will make it so much worse. When you don't have self-discipline not to scratch it, you spread it around with your fingertips. It moves from the back of your hand, all up your arm; it shows up on your cheek; it gets inside your eye. In Lent we allow ourselves to be bitten by mosquitoes so that we can practice not scratching while the itch is fairly mild so that we will be able to resist scratching when the itch is almost unbearable.

So what is this bad case of poison ivy for which we prepare in Lent? What is the real temptation for which we're rehearsing? Matthew provides an answer.

Now I know we've all heard sermons on the story of Jesus's temptation that look at each temptation separately. First, there's the temptation to turn stones into bread. Second, if he were to jump down from the steeple on top of the temple in Jerusalem, God would prevent him from even stubbing his toe and everyone would believe. And third, Satan promises that if Jesus worships him for just a moment, he will give to him authority over all the kingdoms of the world. Physical desire, the quest for power, and the lure of glory. Heck, it's a ready-made three-point sermon if I've ever heard one in my life. All preachers have to do is add two jokes and a poem, and they're ready to fly.

But actually, to walk through each movement of the story and separate them out as different temptations is to risk not seeing Jesus's wilderness for the trees. The three different tests are really only different on the surface. Down deep where the soul is touched, there is only one temptation—one temptation that manifests itself in millions of different ways.

Listen to the first words the Tempter speaks to Jesus, *"Since you are God's Son . . ."* Those words echo back to Jesus's baptism, where the spirit of God descends upon him, and the voice from heaven says, *"This is my Son whom I dearly love; I find happiness in him."* Immediately upon hearing these words at baptism, Jesus is led by the Spirit into the wilderness. And the next words he hears are, *"Since you are God's Son, command these stones to become bread."* The second temptation begins exactly the same way: *"Since you are God's Son, throw yourself down [from the temple]."*

This is my Son . . . Since you are God's Son . . .

The focus here isn't so much on satisfying hunger or on performing miracles for show or on gaining political power as it is on the temptation for Jesus to act in a way that denies his identity as God's child. Of course, Matthew uses the title "God's Son" not just to speak of Christ's divine origins, but also to refer to his divine mission, because Jesus's identity and mission can't be separated. Jesus comes from God as God's child *in order to* serve God's people. Jesus is to meet the hungering needs of those whom society is either unable or unwilling to help. Jesus is to confront those religious authorities who are more concerned with the religious institution than with compassion and justice. Jesus is to preach about the dominion of God over against the dominions of the world in a way that calls those willing to hear the message to a posture of repentance. Jesus is to suffer, die, and be raised for those who follow, for those who forsake, for those who are forlorn, and for those who need forgiveness. The temptation Jesus faces in the wilderness is to turn away from the calling he received in his baptism.

114

This is what God gets angry about if we pass through our baptism and fail to notice: that God calls us. In theological lingo the word is *vocation*, but when we hear that we usually think about career choices. Vocation in the church isn't about *what* you want to be when you grow up; it's about *who* God calls us to be in every moment of our existence—at work, at school, at home, at church, at the gas station, at the basketball game, at the quilting bee . . . well, you get the idea. In baptism God calls us to the vocation of being Christian everywhere and all the time. Temptation doesn't simply challenge what we are going to do in this or that circumstance. It's not just: Am I going to cheat on my taxes, cheat on my spouse, cheat on my homework? Temptation makes us question who we are . . . or better, *whose* we are. Temptation challenges us to cheat on being Christian, to cheat our very God-given identity.

In baptism God speaks to us and says, *"You are my child."* This is both claiming and calling for Christians. But it's not that God only says it once. It echoes through every prayer we utter when we believe God cares: "You are my child." It echoes through every sermon you hear preached in this place: "You are my child." It echoes through the Lord's Supper: "This is my body. This is my blood. *You* are my child." Thank heavens we have heard God claim and call us.

[With a tone of sarcasm] I say, "thank heavens," because once we've heard it, once we know it, once we believe it, once we choose to wear the label "Christian," we are protected from ever being tempted again. That's right: we Christians are never again tempted the way the rest of the human race is tempted. Being persons of faith protects us from real, root-level temptation. After all, we will never be tempted in a time of economic recession to be concerned about our well-being while neglecting the needs of those who are poor and hungry. *If you are a child of God, then . . .* We'll never be tempted to determine our self-worth by how much money we make or what grades we earn or who we marry or what job title we have. *If you are a child of God, then . . .* We'll never be tempted to mistake the church building for the church in mission. *If you are a child of God, then . . .* We'll never be tempted to allow our love for our nation to distort our claims about God's love for all God's people. *If you are a child of God, then . . .* We'll never be tempted to laugh at a joke that demeans someone different than us, whether they be gay, or blond, or black, or old, or Jewish. *If you are a child of God, then . . .* We'll never be tempted in our prayers to transform the creator of the universe into a Santa Claus who should be at our beck and call. *If you are a child of God, then . . .* We'll never be tempted to look at the problems that show up on the evening news, and say "I am only one person, what can I do?" *If you are a child of God, then . . .* We will never be tempted to feel jealous of churches that have something we don't or boastful before churches that do not have what we do. *If you are a child of God, then . . .* We will never be tempted to put our family, our job, our school work, our possessions, our church, our love for UK basketball, our bank account, our country, our beliefs, or ourselves before God. *If you are a child of God, then . . .*

We who are called Christian, we whom God calls, are constantly tempted to forget *who we are*, to forget *why we are*, to forget *whose we are*. Lent is not as fun as Christmas—we don't have any Lenten carols. Lent is not as fun as Easter—no Lenten sunrise services. But we need Lent. We need time to rehearse with small temptations, so that we are ready when louder, more persuasive temptations come along. We need Lent to remind us of our daily vocation of being a Christian. We need Lent to help us notice once again and strive to live out the promise implicit in God saying to each of us every moment of our lives, *"You are my child with whom I am well pleased."*

Parker Palmer tells a story about how similar the voices of temptation and the voice of God sound when it comes to defining who and whose we are.[6] Since the beginning of his adult career, he had had people telling him that someday he would be a college president. One day the opportunity finally came. A school made him an offer, but before he formally accepted he decided to follow the Quaker tradition of gathering a group of trusted friends to serve as a clearness committee. The way such a committee works in the Quaker tradition is to gather for a few hours in which the committee members ask questions of but give no advice to the person seeking discernment. The thing about it is that Palmer admits that he wasn't really looking for discernment so much as it was a chance to brag a little.

Anyway, the clearness committee began by asking Palmer questions like this: What's your vision for the school? How would you change the curriculum? How will you deal with conflict?

Then someone asked the simple question: "What would you like most about being a college president?" And Palmer began to say things like, "Well, *I wouldn't like* having to give up writing and teaching . . . And I wouldn't like the politics of the job . . . And I wouldn't like glad-handing people so they would give money to the school . . . And I wouldn't like . . ." And the questioner interrupted Palmer and reminded him, "I asked what you *would* like most." And Palmer said, "Yes, I'm working toward that. I wouldn't like having to give up my summer vacations . . . And I wouldn't like having to wear a suit all the time . . . And I wouldn't like . . ." And again the questioner asked, "What would you *like* most?" Parker thought, and all he could come up with was, "Well, I guess what I'd like most is getting my picture in the paper with the word *president* under it."

There followed a long, awkward, painful silence. Finally, the same questioner broke the silence and asked a follow-up question, a baptismal question, a Lenten

---

6. Parker J. Palmer, *Let Your Life Speak: Listening to the Voice of Vocation* (San Francisco: Jossey-Bass, 2000), 44–46.

question: "Parker, can you think of an easier way to get your picture in the paper?"

Clearness committee [hold out one hand]. Lent [hold out other hand]. Temptation practice. Don't pass by purple without noticing. Don't pass by without noticing God calling us to the Christian life. Practice—don't scratch. Remember whose are you.